Jiu Jitsu

History, Traditions, Methods, Knowledge, Philosophy

柔術

1st Edition, 2016
2nd Edition, 2019
3rd Edition, 2020
4th Edition, 2022

ISBN: 978-1-7391049-4-8 – Hardback
ISBN: 978-1-7391049-5-5 – Paperback
ISBN: 978-1-7391049-6-2 – eBook

Preface

Jiu jitsu means different things to different people, depending which style is being practiced, you will see later in this book how this has come to be. For clarity when referring to the Japanese art this book will use the term **jūjutsu.** For the Brazilian art the term **jiu jitsu** is used.

This book is not intended to be a 'how-to' manual for learning jūjutsu. There are many such books already available, and these can serve as an invaluable addition to training. No martial art is learned solely from a book, and there is no substitute for a *sensei*. jūjutsu takes time and repetition to master, with many years of dedicated training, typically at least five years or 1,000 training hours in a traditional style before the student is considered ready to earn the coveted black belt.

This book picks up on all those areas of jūjutsu that can be learned and researched 'off the *tatami*' and outside the *dōjō*. Being fluidly proficient in the techniques of jūjutsu takes time. To truly progress, the student must train in both the mental and the physical sides of the art, with as much realism as can be safely allowed. The pursuit of *mushin* (a flow state of mind), zanshin (a higher awareness) and to be able to act impulsively without having to think consciously about the body's movement is the ultimate aim of any martial artist.

Some chapters of this book will help potential students, who are unsure whether jūjutsu is for them, to be able to make a more informed decision. The book will also be of great use to those looking to achieve higher grades in jūjutsu, to expand their knowledge and educate themselves on the broader concepts such as anatomical awareness, scientific principles, mental preparation and historical perspective.

At the end of the book there is also a black belt theory test that can complement a (traditional) practical black belt grading (belt test). My hope is to provide a foundation or platform which will spark an interest in the reader's research that will lead them deeper into their own path of development and search for self-improvement.

This book acts as a brief whirlwind tour of the main topics surrounding the martial art of jūjutsu and in no way seeks to cover every topic fully, merely giving the reader enough understanding from which they can develop and expand their own knowledge.

For myself, this book has been a means of organising and presenting my research in a way that gives it greater meaning and so others can benefit: my modest contribution to jūjutsu and my fellow students.

For the student earning (or aspiring to) the 'black belt'; you are now the custodian of all those who have gone before and have passed down their knowledge. You have a responsibility to understand and appreciate where this knowledge has come from, and to pass on more than you have taken. This keeps the art alive and applicable to modern times, whilst having the respect and awareness of more than just physical application and excellence.

Throughout this book you will find the use of Japanese terminology and language, this has been done purposely. Japanese is the global language of jūjutsu, this allows students to train all over the world and be able to communicate techniques in a common language. The reader can refer back to the translations section at the end of this book to make sense of any unfamiliar terminology.

During the creation of this book, I have used many sources, all of which are referenced. I have also tried to lay down the facts and give you an opportunity to interpret the content for yourself. 'Facts' are often a matter of opinion or perspective, so please take my facts as they are intended. I have represented them to the best of my ability and intentions, without ego, leaving you to form your own opinions and research further where you feel appropriate.

I hope you enjoy reading this book. If you take something back to the *dōjō* or gym and pass it on, I will have contributed to the understanding and interest of others and my intention will have been fulfilled.

Chapter 1: Summary

まとめ

What is Jūjutsu?

Jūjutsu is an unarmed form of combat first used by the samurai warriors of feudal Japan. It is an all-round martial art that uses striking, blocking, grappling, locking, throwing, ground, submission and weapons techniques. Mol (2001) defines jūjutsu as *"A method of close combat, either unarmed or employing minor weapons that can be used in defensive or offensive ways, to subdue one or more unarmed or armed opponents."*[1]

Jūjutsu is used by police and armed forces around the world and for street self-defence, technique is emphasised over power and strength by using the opponent's force against themselves. The trained *jūjitsuka* (student of jūjutsu) is able to subdue their unprepared, unwitting opponent quickly using only the minimal physical effort required.

The modus operandi for jūjutsu is; **minimum effort for maximum effect** [85].

Figure 1 – Jūjutsu ippon-seoi-nage throw

---

[1] Mol, (2001), *Classical Fighting Arts of Japan*, p.10

Jiu Jitsu, Jū Jitsu or Jūjutsu?

Depending on the reference material used, there are several ways of *writing jūjutsu* in English. As jūjutsu is a Japanese word, the correct kanji is read in *hiragana* (the basic Japanese phonetic script).

Figure 2 – Jūjutsu in kanji

The first English-speaking people to translate the Japanese pronunciation of jūjutsu to English writing did so in several different ways. All of these are equally valid today and refer to the same; *jiu-jitsu, jiu-jutsu, ju-jitsu, jujutsu, ju-jutsu or jujutsu*.

The modern Romanisation from 柔術 would be: **jūjutsu** pronounced: *joo-JOOT-soo*. The Macron or horizonal line above the letter 'u' indicates an elongation in the pronunciation of that letter.

Sadaka Uyenishi, a father of British jūjutsu published the ju jutsu spelling in 1905.

Figure 3 - Sadaka Uyenishi's textbook of ju jutsu (1905)

In this book Japanese styles are referred to as jūjutsu, unless referring correctly to an organisation's name, an author's quotation, and Brazilian styles are referred to as jiu jitsu which differs because of the translation difference from Japanese to English and Portuguese.

In Edwardian Britain (1901 – 1910) the terms *jiu jitsu*, *judo* and *jiu-do* were often interchanged when referring to all Japanese martial arts. This is apparent when reading texts from the period.

Jūjutsu can be literally translated as jū 柔 meaning gentle, flexible, soft or pliable, with jūtsu 術 meaning art, technique, science or skill. It should be noted that before the use *of jū, yawara-jutsu* was a term used to describe all martial practice in Japan. The kanji for *yawara-jutsu* came to be read as *jūjutsu*.

'The gentle art' is the most common translation by other authors, but 'the art of gaining victory by yielding or pliancy' is equally valid.

" ... the name jujutsu was not coined until the early seventeenth century and may have contributed to the use of different terms for what is now generally referred to as jujutsu ... schools would often use combinations of names to refer to their system, or to parts of their system."[2]

In Japanese feudal times (1185–1603), jūjutsu was referred to by several other names including: *yawara, kenpō, hakuda , taijutsu, kogusoko, torite, aikijūjutsu* and *kowani.*

"Ju-Jitsu is but one of the many names by which almost one and the same thing have been connoted; kempō, yawara, kugusoku, kumiuchi ... are all slightly different applications of identical principles."[3]

Uyenishi (1907) describes *kempō* as having more of a killing intent than jūjutsu: "[Kempō,] *a method of killing people, possessed many points of resemblance to ju-jitsu but was totally different in practice, being a system of self-defence against sudden attack with intent to kill and replying thereto in kind ...* [in jūjutsu] *these powers are rarely, if ever, exercised."*[4]

---

[2] Mol, (2001), *Classical Fighting Arts of Japan*, p.17
[3] Harrison, (1932), *The Art of Ju-Jitsu*, p.16
[4] Uyenishi, (1940), *The Textbook of Ju-Jutsu as Practised in Japan*, p.15

Learning Jūjutsu

Jūjutsu techniques are initially learned individually, statically, and without resistance from *uke*. Each move learnt in static form is only designed to illustrate and teach a specific principle. Once the basics are learned, the *uke* can attack with more intent, realism and randomisation. An analogy often used to illustrate this point is writing: letters must be learned before sentences which are learned before paragraphs.

Not every technique works on every person or in every situation, so one of the signs of a more proficient *jūjutsuka* is the ability to move fluidly from one technique to another until the opponent, or attack, is neutralised.

Just as learning Japanese terminology is part and parcel of jūjutsu training, counting inside the dōjō is often in Japanese. The basic numbers are shown in Table 1.

Table 1 – Counting in Japanese

1	Ichi	(ee-chee)
2	Ni	(nee)
3	San	(sahn)
4	Shi	(shee)
5	Go	(goh)
6	Roku	(loh-koo)
7	Shichi	(shee-chee)
8	Hachi	(hah-chee)
9	Ku	(kyoo)
10	Juu	(joo)
100	Hyaku	(hya-ku)

As a battlefield art, jūjutsu must be practiced with care and restraint. Its *bujutsu* origins do not lend its potential to sport particularly well. Genuine application of technique will result in serious injury or death; therefore it is not something that can ever be practiced fully outside of a combat or genuine self-defence situation.

The probability is most *jūjutsuka* will never properly use the techniques that they have been taught in the *dōjō*. Jūjutsu gives the student a confidence in themselves just knowing the techniques are there, ready, even if they are not physically used.

Age is no barrier to jūjutsu, using Kanō (the founder of *jūdō* 1860-1938) as an example:

"I have not yet forgotten the truly extraordinary demonstration given many years ago by Dr Jigoro Kano, then the highest-ranking of the native Japanese leaders of Jujitsu. Dr Kano displayed an activity, a force and astonishing accuracy of balance, movement and timing, that would have been highly credible in a man of half his years."[5]

Dr Masaaki Hatsumi (1931) (ninjitsu) and Helio Gracie (1913-2009) (Brazilian jiu jitsu) are 21st century examples of how techniques learnt over a long period can overcome the physical age of the student, both training into their 90s. As youth and strength fade, experience and technique come to fill their place.

Each jūjutsu technique can be applied in more than one situation, often not the scenario in which it was taught. The advanced practitioner combines several principles from their static knowledge to develop a bespoke, fluid response to any attack.

"Even in practice, one should try to imagine one's opponent an actual enemy. A correct posture should be carefully maintained, and the rules of; genshin (the power to anticipate an attack) and of zanshin (how to act after throwing one's opponent) must also be observed... When one is attacked with a wooden sword, one's fear or caution is not great; on the other hand, substitute a steel sword for the wooden one, and caution will be exercised. Let the pupil, then, try to imagine that his opponent is [always] armed with a real sword."[6]

Jūjutsu is taught in stages. First the student learns the basics and then, the more advanced techniques, with the belt system helping to facilitate gradual progression.

Often the earlier belts are more difficult to attain as there is no prior knowledge or precedent to refer back to. The learning mindset should be that jūjutsu is a lifetime's work. To rush for belts just creates bad habits that will hinder progress later on; *"there will be a real tendency among the more in-cautious readers to*

---

[5] Garrud, (1947), *The Complete Jujitsuan*, p.x
[6] Harrison, (1932), *The Art of Ju-Jitsu*, p.21

ignore the earlier tricks, and to take up with the much more advanced ones [but] *to take those up at once may cause injury or death.*"[7]

Jūjutsu can instill values and discipline. Students' self-confidence can also be improved through jūjutsu practice, its close-contact nature can help to cure inhibitions. Jūjutsu can be trained daily by phantoming techniques, by shadow practice, or by the student running through all they have learned mentally, thus making the best use of the limited time in the *dōjō*. The component parts of jūjutsu common to most *ryū* are shown in Table 2.

Table 2 - Umbrella techniques of jūjutsu

Tachi-waza	Stances
Ukemi-waza	Break falling
Atemi-waza	Striking
Nage-waza	Throwing
Ne-waza	Ground work
Katame-waza	Locking, strangling and choking
Kensetsu-waza	Joint manipulation
Kappō	Revival techniques (first aid)
Bu-jutsu	Weapons techniques
Kata	Pre-set routines

It is good practice for the jūjutsu student to learn slowly and master a handful of techniques. Six or seven techniques that can be applied consistently, with speed and on pure 'muscle memory', are far better than thirty or fourty techniques that are performed hesitantly and lack pressure testing.

The principle of giving-way and utilising the antagonist's strength, direction of force and weight against themselves is central to jūjutsu methodology.

'Muscle memory' is a term used to describe when the body's reaction occurs without conscious thought. A good example is braking in the car: when a new driver is learning to drive they have to think about it, after many hours of practice the muscle memory reacts subconsciously.

Constant practice results in automated responses (muscle memory) so the *jūjutsuka* can react on autopilot. Poor training will tune the autopilot to a poor

---

[7] Hancock & Higashi, (1938), *The Complete Kano Jiu-Jitsu*, p.xv

response, so training must always be as realistic as possible and carried out under pressure to best reflect reality. In the *jūjutsuka's* mind, it must always be for real.

"Jujutsu tricks and holds are very simple. A thorough knowledge of them, gained only with constant practice, should develop in one a feeling of strong self-confidence. This confidence causes the jujutsu expert to react almost instinctively in the event of a sudden attack and to manoeuvre the situation to his own advantage (Yoshida)."[8]

There is no short-cut to becoming proficient at jūjutsu; this is no different with most physical skills. As Bruce Lee famously said: *"I fear not the man who has practiced 10,000 kicks once, but I fear the man who has practiced one kick 10,000 times."*

William Fairbairn (1885-1960) was reputedly involved in over 600 real hand-to-hand encounters, his advice carries the weight of someone with a high degree of martial experience:

"Do not consider yourself an expert until you can carry out every movement instinctively and automatically … first, practice every movement slowly and smoothly. Then gradually increase speed until every movement can be executed with lightning rapidity."[9]

One of the most intensive forms of jūjutsu practice is to study as an *uchideshi*. An *uchideshi* is a live-in student (typically in Japan) who lives and sleeps in the *dōjō*, typically for an entire year or more. They clean and do practical work for the *sensei* as well as being an on-demand *uke* in return for daily instruction and a place to stay.

Finding a Dōjō

A critical aspect in all martial arts is finding a club/gym where you enjoy training. The most important thing about the club is the *sensei*. William Bankier's (1870-1949) advice over 100 years ago still stands today:

"I would also wish to guard the student of Ju-Jitsu against Empirics, men who presume upon some qualification or other that is gained at the outset by financial considerations rather than ability. The market is flooded with this class of expert,

---

[8] Nakae, (1958), *Jiu Jitsu Complete*, p.7
[9] Fairbairn, (1924), *Get Tough!*, p.vi

whose theory outruns his practical knowledge in the race for filthy lucre and notoriety."[10]

Jūjutsu takes a great deal of commitment, time, money and personal sacrifice. The student must make sure they are fully comfortable with the *dōjō* and *sensei* before beginning a long term training commitment. Realising a year later there was a more suitable club in the student's area will not only be a waste of time but could also lead to a foregoing many years of training, or quitting before the student had the opportunity to appreciate the effect martial arts could have in their life.

Potential students should visit a number of clubs, watch a training session, speak to other students and be prepared to travel for training. Ask about seminars and interaction with other clubs, this is a great way to broaden understanding and experience. Students should aim to attend at least one seminar every year, even if not directly related to their club, association or style. This communal knowledge over the course of a lifetime's training will make them a much better martial artist.

Whilst on the jūjutsu journey students should avoid the temptation to see the 'black belt' as the ultimate goal; in reality the black belt is the start of a journey, not the end. In a real encounter, the belt worn in class will not do any benefit on the street. Consider the following scenario:

---

[10] Bankier, (1905), *Ju-Jitsu, What It Really Is*, p.13

Figure 4 – Self-defence based on the body's 'acute stress response'

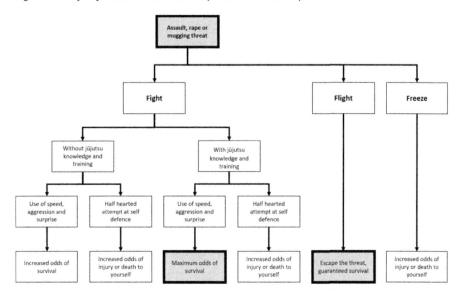

As you can see from Figure 4, survival is first dependant on your 'acute stress response' of **fight**, **flight** or **freeze**. If you can run away then survival is guaranteed, this is why the first rule of self-defence is "**don't be there**."[1]

Training the mind in simulation of a threat, with as much pressure and reality as possible, will help to give more control over the acute stress response when it happens. A well trained threat response will keep the heart rate and breathing under control and allow the body, training, technique and muscle memory to work to maximum effect.

Another way of teaching the acute stress response is to use the formula:

Event + Reaction = Outcome

In Figure 4 the event could be an assault, rape or mugging threat. This event has already arisen and cannot be changed. The six possible outcomes in Figure 4 are also fixed in their increase or decrease of the victim's chances of survival. Regular and realistic training guides the acute stress response into an outcome where the odds of survival can work in the victim's favour not to their detriment.

Nothing is guaranteed in a real encounter, but the object of the exercise is always to increase the odds in the victim's favour. Increasing the chance of survival by just 1% might just be the thing that saves someone's life.

Training without realism or pressure is unlikely to increase the odds of survival; it may well do the opposite. Of course, this depends on why the student wants to learn jūjutsu in the first place, as a keep fit and social activity, as means of self-defence, or as a bit of both. The point is that training and mindset should reflect what the student wants the outcome of their hard work and time to be.

One must train the way they intend to fight.

Sensei

Before c1500, swordsmanship and combat were taught to Japanese *samurai* by the most skilled practitioners working for their *daimyō*. The lessons this skilled warrior had learnt himself (during actual combat) would compound his own experience and be passed down to others within the clan.

With the 1603 unification of Japan under one *shōgun*, battlefield combat declined and fighting moved from full military scale, down to individual encounters. Martial arts teaching for the *samurai* class moved to organised *ryū's*, and the now-familiar student/master relationship began to establish itself. Before 1868 the *samurai* were a distinct social class to the rest of Japan, they were the only members of society permitted to learn jūjutsu and the martial arts.

The head of each *ryū* was the *sensei* (translated as teacher, mentor or master). After the modernisation of Japan following the Meiji restoration in 1868, *dōjōs* became available to all classes of Japanese society rather than just the *samurai* class. Training emphasis at this time moved from pure combat effectiveness to include philosophical training and social etiquette.

Today's *sensei* is just one link in a long chain going back to feudal Japan. The *samurai* of feudal Japan are *"remembered in the history of succeeding generations as a symbol of honour and loyalty, respecting a concept which, nowadays, is quite obsolete; giri."*[11]

A *sensei's giri* (duty) is to keep the link between those who preceded him or her, and those who will follow. In this way, jūjutsu knowledge is passed on to the next generation, with each new *sensei* standing on the shoulders of their forebears.

---

[11] Galan, (2014), *Ju-jitsu as a Method of Psycho-Physical Training in the Contemporary Age*, p.1

Tori and Uke

Tori's (the defender's) role in practice is to ensure the safety of *uke* (the attacker) during the application of a technique. *Tori's* technique is improved through repetition from *uke's* attack.

Uke prepares *tori* by allowing them to practice with increasing levels of resistance, speed, realism and intent. Working with different *ukes'* gives *tori* a greater range of possibilities and variation in training. It also helps to give greater preparation for a real encounter, where the characteristics of each attack will vary from person to person. In jūjutsu training, the student will divide their time equally between playing the roles of *tori* and *uke*.

Figure 5 – Jūjutsu body drop (variation) throw. Tori on the right.

Chapter 2: History

The Samurai

Samurai were the nobility and military officer class of feudal Japan.

"On the fifth day of May –the fifth month- of his fifth year, a samurai child received his sword. They never parted till he went to the crematorium to join his ancestors."[12]

The Japanese word *bushi* meaning 'to wait upon' or 'to accompany', is a generic term for the Japanese warrior, often misinterpreted to refer solely to *samurai*. The *bushi* represented many kinds of warriors, sub-categorised according to social status or the immediate needs of the *shōgun*. The translation of *samurai* being 'one who serves'.

The term *rōnin* was used to describe a *samurai* without a master or lord. *Rōnin* translates as 'wave man' and expresses a drifter, vagrant or wanderer- one who is socially adrift.

"The samurai became accepted as a certain kind of warrior, a 'classical warrior', of great skill, and it is from this background that the samurai trained the warriors in actual combat. The rigorous disciplines prepared the warrior to confront his enemies without fear, knowing full well that the technical and psychological training that he had received enabled him to be in full control of himself and the situation."[13]

The *samurai's* primary weapon was the sword. A symbol of the *samurai* was to wear two swords of different lengths, the *katana* or *tachi* being the longer sword with the *wakizashi* being the shorter sword. The *tantō* (dagger) being shorter still (Figure 27). The combination of wearing two swords is called *daishō* (translated as 'big and small'). During the Edo period (1603-1868), only the *samurai* class were allowed to wear *daishō*.

The primary martial art of the *samurai* was typically *kenjutsu* (swordsmanship). The secondary art was typically jūjutsu: *"... the grappling arts were by no means less important than, or technically inferior to, such armed arts as kenjutsu."*[14]

---

[12] Gluck, (1973), *Zen Combat*, p83.
[13] Clark & Morris, (1985), *Samurai Budo*, p.13
[14] Mol, (2001), *Classical Fighting Arts of Japan*, p.71

Japanese combat arts (or *jutsu*) took many forms; the *samurai* would have trained and been efficient in a host of armed and unarmed combat methods, all referred to as *bujutsu*. *'Bu'* referring to militarisation, and *'jutsu'* referring to a technique.

Table 3 – Bujutsu techniques of the samurai

Armed			Unarmed
Major	Minor	Collateral	
Archery	War fan	Small iron weapons	Jūjutsu
Spearmanship	Staff	Occult arts	
Swordsmanship	Jitte		
Horsemanship			
Swimming			

"Beside learning how to wield their swords aright all bushi underwent instruction in archery, the use of the halberd and lance, and in jujutsu; while many were, also, taught how to handle a boat, to swim, and to ride a horse. How to keep their weapons in order, how to bear pain, heat and cold, starvation and thirst."[15]

Samurai were trained in hand-to-hand combat under their clan schools of jūjutsu. The sword was always the primary weapon of the *samurai*. Much like the rifle is the primary weapon of the modern soldier. If a *samurai* were to lose his sword or find it more convenient at close range to use jūjutsu, then he would have had the required level of proficiency to do so.

"Ju jitsu is the art which every samurai under the feudal regime was compelled to learn, and it was often a point of honour among the higher-minded ones, if attacked by a vulgar opponent, whether with or without a weapon, to try first to overcome him by means of ju jitsu before drawing their own swords."[16]

The *yumi* (longbow) was an earlier primary weapon for a Japanese warrior, being of asymmetric shape so it could be fired from horseback as well as being coupled with a *tate* (shield) whilst on foot. *Samurai* were also proficient with the use of pole weapons such as the *yari* (spear). The *yari* was more commonly used by ordinary foot soldiers called *ashigaru*.

---

[15] Norman, (1905), *The Fighting Man of Japan*, p.3
[16] Harrison, (1950), *The Fighting Spirit of Japan*, p.33

The *samurai* wore armour (known as *yoroi*) which was made of individual iron or leather scales bound together with silk or lace to form the complete armour. A *samurai* would also wear a helmet (*kabuto*). As numbers of *samurai* clans began to rise, their skill sets expanded and steadily they began to filter into senior military and governmental positions. Through the passage of time and alliances between the *samurai*, the first Japanese *samurai*-led government was formed around 1160.

The arrival of US Navy steamships in 1853 forced Japan to open their closed society to trade with Western nations. Over the next 20 years Japan raced to modernise and create a Western-style military force using modern technology.

In 1873 Emperor Meiji abolished the *samurai's* right to be the only armed force in the land, in favor of a Western-style conscripted army carrying firearms. With the *Meiji* reforms in the late 19th century, the *samurai* class and the feudal system were officially abolished and left to decay as a relic of the past. The new imperial Japanese armies consisted of conscripts. A lot of *samurai* volunteered for service and were trained as officers in the new modern army.

Figure 6 – Samurai (with daishō) applying a jūjutsu shoulder lock

Bushidō

The *samurai* followed a set of values referred to as *bushidō*. Translated as 'the way of the warrior,' *bushidō* was the moral code the *samurai* lived by.   This was, however, more than just a warrior code, and to the *samurai bushidō* was a way of life (and death). From the earliest times, the *samurai* recognised their path as one of honour, a duty to one's master and loyalty unto death; this was the way of *bushidō*.

The knights of medieval Europe would have felt a similarity with *samurai bushidō* with their moral code of 'chivalry'. *"...the inspirations of Bushidō, that in Japan means the very best and the very highest form of morality and philosophy... their [the Japanese] code of knightly chivalry is the pure fulfilment of a lofty spirit."*[17]

A notable part of the *samurai* code of honour was the practice of *seppuku* or *hara kiri* (a more vulgar term) which allowed a disgraced *samurai* to regain his honour by committing suicide via self-disembowelment with his own sword.

The brutality and violence in a *samurai's* life were offset to some degree by following *bushidō*, itself influenced by *Shintō* and *Zen* Buddhism. The moral values of the *samurai* and *bushidō* included loyalty, frugality, mastery of oneself (and martial art) and honour (until death).

Bushidō has eight values; righteousness, courage, benevolence, respect, sincerity, honour, loyalty and self-control. A *shisei* (person of moral integrity) is one who adheres to the path of *bushidō*.

---

[17] Bankier, (1905), *Ju-Jitsu, What it Really Is*, p.20

Bujutsu and Budō

Bujutsu

Bujutsu refers to a martial 'art', 'military science', or 'military strategy'. *Bujutsu* is an umbrella term for all warrior-based Japanese martial arts with the only output to be for use in actual combat. *Bujutsu* training prepared the *samurai* technically and psychologically to remain in full control whilst confronting death.

Bujutsu was the forerunner for the later schools of *budō*. It is important to note there is a distinction between the martial 'arts of *bujutsu*' and the martial 'ways of *budō*'. *Bujutsu* is the warrior art, *budō* is the warrior way.

Early classical jūjutsu (794-1603) as practiced by the warring *samurai* is a type of *bujutsu*.

"The emphasis in classical bujutsu was on a spirit of practical realism in techniques, based on the need to apply them in real combat, probably to the death" [18] *"...conditions for their genesis have disappeared".*[19]

"The bujutsu are combative systems designed by and for warriors to promote self-protection and group solidarity. The budō are spiritual systems, not necessarily designed by warriors or for warriors, for self-protection of the individual."[20]

Budō

Budō is a martial 'way' and is common to more modern Japanese martial arts. Practitioners are not necessarily full-time warriors anticipating to face death as a profession and may concentrate on spiritual development as much as effective competence in battle. There is a move away from the killing of bujutsu into the more humane application of technique.

"[Bujutsu] ... is particually related to the practical, technical and strategic aspects of these arts ... when these specilizations are intended as disciplines with an end of purpose of a more educational or ethical nature, 'technique' [Jitsu] becomes 'way' (do) meaning the 'path' toward a spiritual rather than purely practical achievement."[21]

---

[18] Goodger (1981), *The Development of Judo in Britain*, p.21
[19] Goodger (1981), *The Development of Judo in Britain*, p.17
[20] Draeger, (1973), *Classical Bujutsu*, p.19
[21] Ratti and Westbrook, (2009), *Secrets of the Samurai*, p.35

Jūjutsu can be both a type of *bujutsu* and *budō*. Often the difference is disputed by the practitioner on the basis of history, training methods, philosophy and spiritual development. *Bujutsu* having a more martial and combative intent whereas *budō* errs towards a more philosophical emphasis.

Table 4 – Differences between bujutsu and budō

	Translation	Intent	Jūjutsu Period
Bujutsu	Warrior art	To kill	Early classical (794-1603)
Budō	Warrior way	Journey for self-improvement	Late classical and traditional (1603-1926)

Historical Periods of Japan

Table 5 – Historical periods of Japan inc martial arts and jūjutsu periods

	Paleolithic (c35,000 BC–14,000 BC)	
	Jōmon (14,000–300 BC)	
	Yayoi (300 BC–250 AD)	
	Kofun (250–538)	
	Asuka (538–710)	
	Nara (710–794)	
Japanese ***Koryū*** Martial Arts	Heian (794–1185)	**Early Classical Jūjutsu Period**
	Kamakura (1185–1336)	
	Muromachi / Ashikaga (1336–1573)	
	Azuchi-Momoyama (1568–1603)	
	Edo / Tokugawa (1603–1868)	**Late Classical Jūjutsu Period**
Japanese ***Gendai*** Martial Arts	Meiji (1868–1912)	**Traditional Jūjutsu Period**
	Taishō (1912–1926)	
	Shōwa (1926–1989)	**Modern Jūjutsu Period**
	Heisei (1989–2019)	
	Reiwa (2019-Present)	

There is no common agreement among historians on exactly when each Japanese historical period began and finished. Furthermore, some periods carry different names and often sub-sections named after each reigning Emperor. The above list should thus be used a 'brief' guide. The different jūjutsu periods and their styles are explained later in this chapter.

The History of Jūjutsu

It is impossible to study the history of jūjutsu without concurrently looking at the history of Japan. The previous section on 'historical periods of Japan' will help to gain a chronological overview of the evolving history of jūjutsu.

Jūjutsu is over 1,500 years old, forged from the trial and error, death and suffering of thousands of practitioners. Its exact origins have been lost in the passage of time and antiquity. Traditionally, jūjutsu knowledge was passed down orally (and of course physiologically) from teacher to student, generation after generation. Owing to the lack of documentation, there are gaps in history that may never be accurately filled.

In Japanese mythology, the gods Kajima and Kadori are said to have used jūjutsu to discipline the lawless inhabitants of the eastern provinces.

Figure 7 – World map showing position of Japan

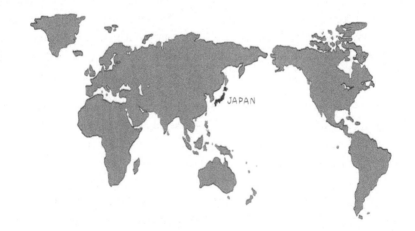

Figure 8 – Map of Japan

Japan is a mountainous country consisting of four separate islands: Hokkaidō, Honshū, Shikoku and Kyūshū. Historically, the mountainous terrain made agriculture difficult, which also made it very complex for a centralised government to rule. Smaller self-governing states were formed, leading to skirmishes and fighting over the limited amount of fertile lands within the Japanese islands.

The earliest traces of Japanese civilisation can be found in the *Kofun* burial mounds where the *uji* (leaders of the earliest known tribes) were buried. The most important *uji* claimed descent from Jimu Tennō, the great-great-grandson of the sun goddess Amaterasu. This warrior king became the first emperor of Japan and established Japan's first capital city at Nara. His ancestral line then became the Japanese imperial family. Although not regarded as living gods, the Japanese emperors were regarded with awe and reverence by the population.

Far from the capital, the smaller self-governing remote states of Japan needed to be brought under central rule. Emperor Suijin (at a date thought to be between 97 BC and 300 AD) granted a commission for a single military commander, called a *shōgun*, to take charge of all his military forces, and reign in the rogue states. The rank of *shōgun* was supposed to be surrendered on completion of this task.

Provincial communities grew up around warrior families who were known as *bushi dan*. These families extended to unrelated young warriors referred to as *kenin* and allegiance was to the *uji* of the clan. The emperor stayed in power by consent from these *uji* (clan) chiefs who would often rebel and have to be put down by amassing a force enlisted by the emperor's government from provincial lords called *daimyō* and their private armies.

" ... *Until the time of the Hojo regime (say from the twelfth to the fourteenth century) no special [jūjutsu] school had developed. Later, however, the various methods employed by physically inferior persons in defeating physically superior antagonists were carefully elaborated, until eventually many distinct ryugi, sects or schools came into existence.*"[22]

From around the year 900 to 1603, Japan was in a state of almost constant civil war. A warrior could spend his whole life on the battlefield. Fighting was a life's work for a Japanese warrior and perfecting his proficiency in battle was a reason for living. In an age of close combat, weapons to empty handed systems of fighting, as well as defending against weapons and defending unarmed and multiple attackers, was commonplace. Hand-to-hand battles would often be fatal, with the victor being able to learn and refine their technique for their next encounter.

The Japanese tribal clans in the Heian period (794-1185) were connected politically and economically in much the same way as witnessed during the Middle Ages in Europe. The *daimyō* were the landowners and ruling class of Japan. In times of war, power drifted from the emperor to the *shōgun* and down to the *daimyōs*. The imperial Kyoto government gradually became weaker through this transfer of power.

The bow was the most advanced weapon of the (pre-Heian [794]) time and the hired warriors of the *daimyō* were proficient in horse riding and archery. These hired warriors were given privileged status by their local *daimyō* in exchange for their services. A *daimyō's* hereditary warriors were called *bushi* who had status and prestige, which related to the domain their *daimyō* governed. The *bushi* took on their own students who later became warriors in their own right.

During the reign of Emperor Ninmyo (833-856), documented evidence can be found referring to an annual martial arts contest of two distinct grappling forms. The first sporting form was for competitors bred to wrestle in what became known

---

[22] Harrison, (1932), *The Art of Ju-Jitsu*, p.15

as *sumō*. The second form was for warriors to grapple combatively to maintain the advantage in combat. This would later become known as jūjutsu.

A *bushi's* student retainers were commonly horsed archers and squires who, over time, became a noble class known as *samurai* (translated literally as 'one who serves'). Larger-scale warfare led to the sword and spear becoming more preeminent. Usage of the bow was reduced and eventually the sword became the *samurai's* primary weapon.

The *samurai* chose to pursue a life of warfare guided by a code of conduct known as *bushidō* (the way of the warrior).

To put the *samurai* in a Western context, the knights of medieval Europe worked and lived on values of 'chivalry' in a similar way to the *samurai* having their values of *bushidō*.

Feudalism is a social hierarchy where aristocratic and military governmental rule are the dominant controlling force over land ownership, resulting in power and control over the population.

From around 400 to 1300 in Europe, and between 700 and 1868 in Japan, feudalism took hold across the two cultures. This developed in total independence, yet with striking similarities as shown in Table 6.

Table 6 – Feudal comparison of society between Japan and Europe

Japan	Role in Society	Europe
Emperor	**Religious or spiritual leader**	Pope
Shōgun	**Political leader**	Monarch
Daimyō	**Landowners**	Nobles
Samurai / Rōnin	**Soldiers**	Knights
Peasants	**Highest commoner**	Merchants
Artisans	**Middle commoner**	Craftsmen
Merchant	**Lowest commoner**	Peasants

Figure 9 – Japanese feudal pyramid

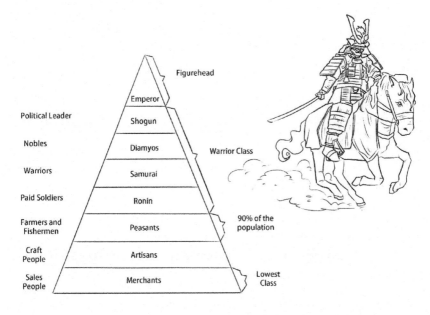

Figure 10 – European feudal pyramid

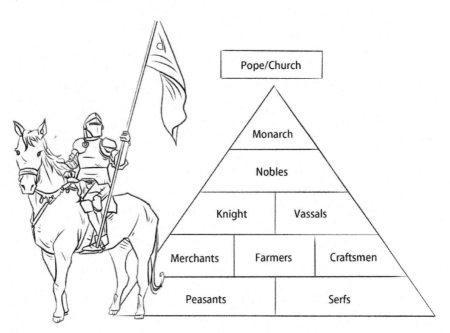

The *samurai* in Japan were akin to the knights of Europe. Lewis (1974) notes that *"Despite considerable scholarly research, however it still remains unclear whether the feudal systems which produced these warriors, truly resemble each other although they obviously have a large measure of superficial similarity."*[23]

The Japanese armour for the *samurai* was developed to be light and offer greater maneuverability, whilst the European armour for the knight concentrated on size and weight.

Private *samurai* armies became so strong that some *daimyo* were capable of avoiding taxation and military service, with the imperial household having to hire their own *samurai* to resist the power of the *daimyō*.

During the 12th century the two non-governmental leading Japanese warrior clans; the Minamoto and the Taira, fought for control of the emperor and to rule Japan. *"In 1180 the two great clans met head-on in the Gempei war, a bitter and ferocious affair that was to last five years."*[24]

In 1185, the Minamoto triumphed and Yoritomo Minamoto (1147-1199) became Japan's first permanent *shōgun* in 1192. Ending the Heian period. Yoritomo's military government increased its authority until it overshadowed the Imperial court and the emperor. Yoritomo built the loyalty of the provincial *daimyō*'s by rewarding their service with gifts of land. *"This was the first government recorded in Japanese history that was staffed almost entirely by professional warriors."*[25]

"After he had been granted an official sanction by the sovereign to become Japan's first permanent shogun, or generalissimo, Yoritomo became the powerful martial arm of the sovereign and the protector of the imperial court; he was, in fact, the absolute ruler of Japan."[26]

The *samurai* became the ruling class of Japan, all *daimyō* were now also from *samurai* stock. As a noble class, they could focus all their time and effort into the practice of warfare. Fighting skills were passed on in families and from father to son as a privilege of their nobility. Although few *ryū* gave prominence to grappling during the twelfth and thirteenth centuries, a few schools were beginning to

---

[23] Lewis, (1974), *Knights & Samurai*, p.1
[24] Fairhurst, (1991), *Ju Jutsu – The Science The Art*, p.2
[25] Draeger, (1973), *Classical Bujutsu*, p.17
[26] Draeger, (1973), *Classical Bujutsu*, p.25

specialise in this secondary form of combat as a supplementary system to their weapons techniques.

Later *shōguns* (in the Hōjō and Ashikaga periods 1185-1573) proved to be less competent than Yoritomo at keeping the peace; anarchy prevailed and the *daimyō* began to once again war with each other. To bolster their forces the *daimyō* took on a new class of warrior in addition to *bushi* (trained warriors) paying *nobushi* (field warriors) or *ashigaru* (light-footed soldiers) to bolster their ranks. These men had neither the means nor birthright to join the higher ranks of the *bushi* and so offered their services in return for adventure and guaranteed employment, their proficiency being as varied as their loyalty. The *daimyō* also conscripted *ji-samurai* (farmer-warriors) who could be called upon to drop their farming tools and fight when required.

During the Muromachi period (1336-1573) Japanese warriors began to wear armour on the battlefield as protection from the primary weapons of spear, bow and sword. The first armour designs were very heavy and ornate and were designed primarily for horseback. This armour rapidly evolved as the *samurai* developed a lighter version that would be of greater use for field combat and eventually the *hotoke-do* design of *samurai* armour became the most popular. The joints in the armour were concealed and protected against heavy blows from sharp weapons.

Figure 11 – Hotoke-do design of samurai armour

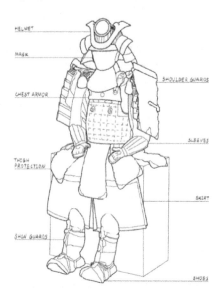

Hand-to-hand striking techniques were largely useless against a *samurai* in armour, and so unarmed grappling techniques of the *samurai* developed with a bias towards throwing, immobilising, locking and choking as well as targeted attacks to the eyes, nose and groin, which could be used against an opponent wearing his full armour.

When in close range with another *samurai* on the battlefield, but considered too close for weapons, the objective would have been to quickly bring the opponent to the ground, using the techniques known as *kumi-uchi*. The *tantō* (dagger) could then be used to slip through a weak point in the *yoroi* (armour) and dispatch the opponent.

Short sticks and daggers were considered within the framework of jūjutsu and could be used effectively against the primary weapons of the attacker. A fully trained, unarmed, or lightly armed warrior could defeat an armed and heavily armoured opponent. The use of these small weapons was effective in this situation in conjunction with the grappling techniques of jūjutsu. The jūjutsu of the Muromachi period (1336-1573) is commonly referred to today as **early classical**

jūjutsu, *yawara, or nihon koryū ju jitsu*. Mol (2001) refers to these older jūjutsu styles as being '*Koryū*' jūjutsu as opposed to 'modern' or 'traditional' jūjutsu.[27]

The *shōgun* of Japan employed vast armies of *samurai* to protect their respective militarised states. By the mid-1400s, the *shōgun* states were in an all-out war with each other, a conflict lasting a further 200 years.

Systems and schools of jūjutsu began to be formulated and documented. Handed down through families and clans these schools were called *ryūha*. Prince Hisamori Takeunochi founded one of the first recorded jūjutsu schools in Japan in 1532. His school 'Hinoshita Toride Kaizan Takenouchi-ryū' jūjutsu was actually only a small part of a wider school which also taught a range of weapon techniques including sword, staff, iron fan and resuscitation methods. Many more *ryū* have been both recorded and lost in history.

The original *ryūha* were designed purely as systems for killing adversaries, and as such most have not survived periods of peacetime. Entire books have been dedicated to the study of these ancient *bujutsu* schools.

Toyotomi Hideyoshi (general, *samurai, daimyō* and politician) united Japan during the Azuchi-Momoyama age (1568–1603). Hideyoshi established new rules of social reform, leading to a birthright class system where the *samurai* were a distinctive separate class representing about 8% of the Japanese population.

Firearms arrived in Japan in the mid-1500s in the form of muskets which caused an uproar with the warrior class as unlike traditional warrior arts, they required very little training to become proficient. The use of firearms was called *hō-jutsu*. The use of firearms was contrary to the established honour of combat.

It was not until the Edo / Tokugawa period (1603-1868) that the term jūjutsu became commonplace within Japan. Before this time, what would be recognised as jūjutsu techniques were referred to by a variety of names shown in Table 7.

Table 7 - Older Japanese terminology for jūjutsu

Kogusoku koshi-no-mawari	Short sword grappling
Kumiuchi	Grappling
Taijutsu	Body art
Yawara	Softness

---

[27] Mol, (2001), *Classical Fighting Arts of Japan*, p.2

Wajutsu yawara- jutsu	Art of harmony
Torite	Catching hand
Jūdō	Way of softness

Jigorō Kanō would later re-use the '*jūdō*' term for *Kōdōkan jūdō*. The terms *yawara*

and *jū* are so similar that they are represented by the same kanji .

The Edo / Tokugawa period was a time of relative peace for Japan, the civil warfare of pre-1603 having been quietened with the uniting of the country under the Tokugawa government. Peace and prosperity were then maintained for over 200 years by the Tokugawa *Shōgunate* who ruled Japan with a chain of 15 continuous *shōguns*. Without a war to fight, the *samurai* class declined, and those who remained took to fighting each other in single combat (sword fighting). In 1650 a law was passed to try and stop this dueling.

As armed warfare became less acceptable (illegal) the hand-to-hand skills of the *samurai* became more preeminent and flourished, this was the 'golden age' of **late classical jūjutsu**. The striking elements of jūjutsu were reintroduced during this period, although mainly as a pre-emptive technique to lead into the throws, locks and strangles. The universal characteristics of jūjutsu remained, focusing on the efficient output of energy, using the opponent's force against themselves and technique over strength and fitness.

At this time, jūjutsu was commonly used in life or death struggles with practices such as the use of blades, chains, biting, eye-gouging, pressure points and brute strength all being deployed. During this period the art of *sekko tsuin* (bone setting) was also a tradition and art practiced by the *samurai*. The Edo period (1603-1869) of flourishing jūjutsu enabled the cataloguing of techniques and subsequent refinements in competition to take place.

Warriors and skilled combatants without an output for their jūjutsu skills would challenge each other to duels, often publicly, to earn a living. Competitions between jūjutsu schools improved techniques and ways of employing them. Encounters were frequently lethal, the survivor's reputation becoming established with each contest and adding to the reputation of the school. The Edo / Tokugawa period, with its many grappling encounters, filtered out ineffective technique and the jūjutsu *ryū* that were found lacking floundered in combat, tested by contests where only the most effective techniques and schools would survive the era.

With the absence of war, teaching jūjutsu became a way for a redundant *samurai* to earn a living. In 1717, in an effort to control the rising number of jūjutsu schools, the *metsuke* (Tokugawan secret police) forced all schools and styles of martial arts to be registered.

Late classical jūjutsu, jūjutsu proper, *koryū* jūjutsu and Edo jūjutsu are terms referring to the style of jūjutsu as practiced in the Edo / Tokugawa period where there was extensive use of *atemi waza* (striking techniques). The Edo techniques were geared more towards street clothing vs. the armoured style of the (early classical) *koryū* period (Japan before 1603).

Estimates from the *Nippon Kobudo Kyokai* (Association of Traditional Japanese Martial Arts) state jūjutsu schools in the Edo period numbered 179. Mol (2001) stated that *"...it is not unreasonable to believe that some three hundred jujutsu ryuha could have existed."*[28]

Up until the penultimate years of the Edo period, Japan was a closed country with a policy of no trade or interaction with the rest of the world. Feudalism had effectively disappeared in Western Europe by about 1500. The Japanese, due to their isolation, were yet to modernise or industrialise.

In 1853, under the command of Commodore Perry, American warships entered the coast of Japan at Uraga near Edo (Tokyo bay). This was the first diplomatic contact Japan had had with the West since the Emperor had dispatched a delegation of *samurai* to Rome in 1613. The Japanese were forced to open their country up to trade and, for the first time, began to connect with the rest of the world, thus releasing the country from its self-imposed exile. After 1853 *"...commerce developed rapidly. Merchants began to have more power than the samurai."*[29]

The last Tokugawa *shōgun*, Keiki, resigned in 1867 leading to the civil war of 1868-1869, and Japan was handed back to Emperor Mutsuhito, who assumed all the *shōgun's* power back for the first time since 1192. This became known as the Meiji Restoration. Power began to drift from the *samurai* class to the new middle classes. Jūjutsu and the martial arts were in a rapid decline.

In 1876 the Japanese government, now keen to be seen as a civilised Westernised country to the *gaijin* (foreigners), passed a law banning the wearing of swords - the

---

[28] Mol, (2001), *Classical Fighting Arts of Japan*.
[29] Dixon, (2003), *Ju-Jitsu*, p.7

very symbol of the *samurai* who were now an obsolete tier of society. It had become proven that a *"...coward armed with a musket could defeat the most courageous and skillful swordsman."* [30] The swordsman and the martial artist (*bushi*) were no longer effective in modern battle.

With the beginnings of Westernisation, the era of the merchant was upon Japan. This reversed Japan's entire social structure and tipped the warrior to the bottom of its social class system, forcing him to become redundant. In 1877, the *samurai* of the Satsuma clan led a rebellion against the *gaijin* and the *Meiji* government. The new imperial Japanese army, comprised of merchants and farmers, managed to defeat the *samurai* using Western weapons in the ensuing bloodbath, the symbolic end of the *bushi*.

Goodger (1981) describes the samurai as being at a definite disadvantage because of their rigid habits and honorable ways of fighting that was restricted to civil battles, their *"Practical fighting efficiency was limited when moving outside of the context in which there were shared assumptions about what 'fighting' was"*.[31] Draeger (1973) describes the classical warrior being replaced by *"the citizen-soldiers of a conscript army in which the classical-warrior type was exceedingly rare."*[32]

Jūjutsu almost died out with the removal of the *samurai*. It was forced underground, considered to be inappropriate for the image that the new Japan wanted to project to the world.

Jūjutsu was now practiced in secret by a smaller number of schools, and commonly used by criminals and street thugs, which did little to promote its image. A small number of techniques survived through the popularity of commercial shows called *gekken kōgyo*, where skilled martial artists could still make a living demonstrating their skills to an audience. Some *samurai* joined the *yakuza* (gangsters), guarding brothels and gambling establishments.

Traditional jūjutsu, *Nihon goshin* jūjutsu and *Gendai* jūjutsu are terms referring to the style of jūjutsu established after the *Meiji* restoration of 1868.

---

[30] Draeger, (1973), *Classical Bujutsu*, p.43
[31] Goodger (1981), *The Development of Judo in Britain*, p.22
[32] Draeger, (1973), *Classical Bujitsu*, p.18

In 1895, the *Dai Nihon Butokukai* was formed to try and keep the martial arts alive. This was the first attempt to organise the martial arts since 1717, when the *Metsuke* police required all martial arts schools to register their instructors.

In 1882, Jigorō Kanō, a master of Tenshin Shin'yō and Kito ryū jūjutsu, developed Kōdōkan jūdō as a socially acceptable alternative to jūjutsu for modern Japanese society.

Kanō was greatly distressed to witness the gradual decline of the martial arts and masters taking techniques to the grave owing to the lack of students. Kanō became involved in education with the Japanese government and in 1882 developed a form of jūjutsu that, as far as possible, occluded risk of injury to its practitioners. His style was taken from a variety of jūjutsu *ryū* and masters. Jūdō, as it would later be known, was a more socially acceptable format of martial arts focusing on the spiritual, intellectual and physical development of its students through physical culture.

In 1900, Kanō's Kōdōkan *jūdōka* contested with the *jūjutsuka* of *Fusen ryū* jūjutsu and failed owing to a lack of groundwork techniques. The Kōdōkan syllabus consequently expanded and reached its current form by 1906. In the same year the formal katas of Kōdōkan jūdō were formulated by 14 jūjutsu masters and six members of the Kōdōkan.

In the 1890's Japanese martial artists began to travel around the world, demonstrating and teaching jūjutsu and jūdō to the western world. American president Roosevelt was instructed by Yamashita Yoshiaki and a Western expert that had trained in Japan Professor John O'Brian who writes in 1906 *"Less than a generation ago you could not have obtained this knowledge at any price. So religiously have the principles of jiu-jitsu been guarded that no foreigner has ever before received official instruction from one who has taken the highest degree in the art".*[33]

Time moved on in Japan, and jūjutsu itself was becoming abundantly unpopular due to the rise of its three new offshoots of jūdō, aikidō and wadō ryū karate. Jūjutsu training required combative experience to hone its practitioner's skills, which was becoming rare in modern society and warfare.

---

[33] O'Brian, (1906), The Japanese Secret Science, p.1

The traditional Japanese arts were driven back again after 1945 and World War II. All martial arts across Japan were banned by the American General MacArthur, who restricted the practice of *budō* and many of the old martial traditions whilst America occupied Japan (1945-1952).

Today jūjutsu has many different styles and variations which combine Japanese classical, traditional and modern style techniques. Many modern schools have also absorbed complementary techniques from other martial arts. It is common practice for *senseis'* to modify and expand on what they have been taught, evolving the techniques to adapt to the changing world and create their own *ryū*.

Some of these modern *ryū* have adapted and modified the older techniques so much that **modern jūjutsu** can vary greatly from one *ryū* to the next. Jūjutsu, however, has always been an evolving art.

As jūjutsu continues to evolve in the West, this Westernised style of jūjutsu is commonly referred to as *gaijin goshin* (foreigner's self-defence) jūjutsu. The techniques are modernising to reflect the areas and society at the time where they are being taught. All styles pay homage to their roots, and most new techniques and variations are easily recognisable as jūjutsu.

The Jūjutsu Schools of Ancient Japan

There are scholars who have written entire books documenting the old jūjutsu *ryū* of Japan. Historical accuracy is beset with difficulty due to the reliability of ancient literature. Therefore, different scholars present varying views as to the facts of when, where, and if, certain schools and people existed.

"The primary purpose of the martial ryu, therefore, was educational in the sense that it involved the transmission of systematic knowledge in the specializations of bujutsu through the use of teaching specialists who were considered capable of producing fighting specialists."[34]

The ancient *ryū's* of Japan (post-1300) committed their history, customs and beliefs onto hand scrolls called *makimono*. Many surviving scrolls are either difficult to decipher or are held in secret and still not accessible to scholars.

The earliest mention of the first jūjutsu school is described by Clark and Morris (1985) as being formed by Miura and Terada who *"formed two separate schools. The art as practiced by Miura was named Wa (the equilavent of Yawara) and the art taught by Terada was named Ju (the equivalent of Ju-Jutsu). The date of this period is unknown, but it is believed to be prior to 1671."*[35]

Arrington (2010) describes the earliest jūjutsu curriculum as being *"...found in the Tenshin Shoden Katori Shinto-ryu, a fifteenth-century martial arts school. These techniques were practiced while wearing full armour and were collectively called Yawara."*[36]

Prior to the Edo / Tokugawa (1603–1868) period, the *ryū* were all-round warrior training schools designed to ensure the survival of their *samurai* on the battlefield. The syllabus would include everything the master knew about survival using whichever weapons were available; forming an all-round martial discipline. Different *ryū*, whilst maintaining a generalised approach, would specialise in the one particular area that was the forte of that particular school. One such school that would become classified as excelling in jūjutsu (or grappling) was the Takeouchi ryū.

---

[34] Ratti & Westbrook, (2009), *Secrets of the Samurai*, p.136
[35] Clark & Morris, (1985), *Samurai Budo*, p.15
[36] Arrington, (2010), *Yawara*, p.11

These 'unarmed' techniques would often include hidden accessories made of iron, such as *tekagi* (spiked gauntlets) or *shuriken* (spikes). This scavenger style martial art that complemented the grappling later to become known as jūjutsu, was called *kakushijutsu*. Certainly the *ninjitsu ryū's*, such as Koga Ninja ryū, Gyokko ryū, Togakure Ninpo ryū and Koto ryū, were actively including these weapons with their 'unarmed' techniques.

Weapons associated with the *Nihon Koryū* (pre-1868) forms of jūjutsu are shown in Table 8.

Table 8 – Weapons associated with ancient Japanese jūjutsu

Shuriken	Spikes
Shaiken	Throwing stars
Jutte	Iron truncheon
Nawa	Rope
*Manriki	kusari*	Weighted chain
Maskari	Axe
Musari-gama	Sickle and chain
Tekken-zu	Iron ring
Kumade	Rake

Some schools of this period would teach unarmed combat to enable the arrest or capture of the enemy or simply to regain the advantage if the warrior's primary weapon was displaced. It should be noted that a warrior losing his sword in battle (as effective as jūjutsu was) would be close to certain death when unarmed and facing a trained swordsman. This is akin to facing down a gun, unarmed, in the modern age; techniques exist but are accepted as a last resort with a high level of failure.

Although records of the early jūjutsu *ryū* are sparse, accounts exist of a warrior named Fukuno who developed techniques of fighting without weapons. His prowess became such that he could defeat much bigger and stronger opponents. His two students, Miura and Terada, went on to teach *wa* (*yawara*) and *jū* (jūjutsu).

Some scholars record that Miura Yōshin, a native of Nagasaki, believed that using the body and mind in unison helped to fight disease and, with the help of two students, went on to develop 51 jūjutsu techniques. The Yoshin ryū (willow hearted) school; was either named because of the suppleness of the willow tree when loaded with snow, or from records of the mysterious master, Yōshin.

Other sources credit Akiyama Shirōbei Yoshitoki as the founder of Yoshin ryū;

"[Yoshitoki] … *a physician of Nagasaki. He had been to China to study and had there learned under one Haku-tei or Pao-chuan three 'te', or tricks, of ju-jitsu… Yoshitoki fully mastered these three 'te' together with twenty-eight different kassei-ho or means of resuscitation… Yoshitoki then sought to improve his art, and it is recorded that he retired to the Temmangu temple at Tsukushi for a hundred days, where he finally succeeded in increasing the number of his 'te' to one hundred and three.*"[37]

The Yoshin ryū trained a student by the name of Tabizaemon Yamamoto, who went on to found the Shin-no-shindo ryū, one of the first schools to introduce a pre-Kanō belt system where beginners would achieve *shodan* (the first grade), followed by *chu-dan* (translated as middle rank) and then finally *jo-dan* (upper rank).

Makimono from the Yoshin ryū, still survive to this day, "*… five scrolls (makimono) relating to a number of masters and practitioners from the Yoshin-ryu school of jujitsu; all have some connection to Kono Suan, the fourth master of this school.*"[38]

It is generally considered that the two ancient schools of Yoshin ryū and Ryoi Shinto ryū were merged by Sekizai Minamoto-ne-Masatari Yanagi. Born in Seishin, he moved to Kyoto at the age of 15 to study jūjutsu for five years under Hitosuyanagi Oride. He founded his style of Tenjin Shin'yō ryū in 1845, translated as 'style utilising the harmony between man and nature' "*and fixed the number of 'te', or tricks, at one hundred and twenty four.*"[39] Yanagi would later change his name to Kuriyama Matayemon and become a retainer of the Tokugawa government. He later changed his name again to Mataemon Iso and died in 1862 with around 5,000 students practicing at his *dōjō*.

Jigorō Kanō would later become a student of Tenjin Shin'yō ryū and go on to found Kōdōkan jūdo based on the styles of Takenouchi ryū, Soshishitsu ryū, Sekiguchi ryū and Kito ryū, later incorporating *Ne-Waza* from Fusen Ryu. "*It* [Tenjin Shin'yō ryu] *was one of the last Koryu jujitsu that was founded before the Meiji restoration. It was created around 1830.*"[40]

---

[37] Harrison, (1932), *The Art of Ju-Jitsu*, p.16
[38] Kuboyama, (2015), *The 'Mind-Set' of Jujutsuka in the Edo period*.
[39] Harrison, (1932), *The Art of Ju-Jitsu*, p.11
[40] Caracena, (2017), *Tenjin Shinyo Ryu JuJitsu*, p.28

The Takenouchi ryū, which is still active to this day, is believed to have been founded by Hisamori, a high ranking *bushi*, systemising techniques so they could be taught in his *dōjō*.

Chinese influence into jūjutsu may have come from Chen-Yuan-Pin (Gempin) who was of Chinese origin or (as some accounts suggest) a *samurai* named Terada. Three *rōnin* students of Gempin, Fukuno Hichiroemon, Isogai Jirozaemon and Miura Yojiemon went on to found the Kito ryū. The Sekiguchi ryū was then founded by Sekiguchi Jushin in the 1600s.

The classical jūjutsu schools of Japan were developed from actual combat experience, and as such, many people argue their teachings are more effective than much younger, more modern schools. In the modern world (unlike ancient Japan) duels to the death to prove or disprove which system or school is more effective are not commonplace.

Modern no-holds-barred contests do of course exist but are bound by rules not found in life-or-death scenarios or on the battlefield. The debate continues, and the student must choose which direction they wish to take based on the outcomes they require from their training.

The History of British Jūjutsu

Jūjutsu found its way to the UK (as records would indicate) as a world first. The first recorded mention was in a lecture by Takashima Shidachi to the London Japan Society in 1892. *"Some might say that wrestling might be compared to ju-jitsu, but the latter is really quite different; the former aims at victory by strength, while the latter gains it by yielding to strength."*[41] Shidach translated ju-jitsu as 'sleight of body' for the audience then proceeded to demonstrate on the English secretary of the society who was thrown around completely untrained in 'evening dress'.[42]

Jūjutsu and its instructors came to Britain as a secondary consequence of the newly industrialising and opening Japan, its business and trade spreading around the world.

British businessmen who had worked with the Japanese, and the British armed forces began to train in jūjutsu, and steadily brought their new skills back to Britain. Ernest John Harrison (1873-1961) is one such example, training in Tenjin Shin'yō ryū whilst working as a journalist in Yokohama around 1897.

During Japan's industrialisation, many Western experts were contracted to the Japanese government. One of these people was a British railway engineer by the name of Edward William Barton-Wright (1861–1951) who had been trained in jūjutsu in Tōkyō. Barton-Wright's 'New Art of Self Defence' based in London, opened to the public in 1899 with a style he named 'Bartitsu'. Jūjutsu was therefore the first oriental martial art to reach British shores.

---

[41] Japan Society (1892), Transactions and Proceedings, p.5
[42] Japan Society (1892), Transactions and Proceedings, p.17

Image 1 – Edward, William Barton-Wright (c1900)[43]

Longhurst (1929) credits Barton-Wright with the introduction of jūjutsu to the UK; *"A Mr. Barton-Wright, an English engineer who had lived for many years in Japan, was responsible for the introduction of this wonderful Japanese system of Self Defence into this country."[44]*

Barton-Wright had invited his Japanese teacher, Master Yukio Tani (1881–1950) of Tenjin Shin'yō ryū jūjutsu along with his brother Kaneo to the Britain to showcase the value of jūjutsu against western boxing, wrestling and circus strongmen. Tani arrived in Britain in 1899 under the ring name 'The Pocket Hercules'.

Two jūjutsu activities were being born in Britain from 1899, (1) active participation largely by small numbers from the middle classes and (2) larger spectator shows attended primarily by the lower classes *"It is clear that, for a period of about fifteen years... jujutsu was established, by a number of Japanese and their English pupils, as an activity undertaken by high-status English individuals an as a spectacle enjoyed by many more, generally of lower status, through the music-halls."[45]*

Percy Longhurst (1874–1959) watched the first of Tani's demonstrations organised by Barton-Wright. *"No one was ready to admit that this novel form of self-defence had a really practical value, though certainly it was difficult to put forward any satisfactory explanation of the evident ease and efficiency which the demonstrator... [Yukio Tani] opposed a first-class professor of the Cumberland and*

---

[43] Breen, (2012), *A History of Ju-Jitsu*.

[44] Longhurst, (1929), *Ju-Jutsu and Judo*, p.5

[45] Goodger, (1989), The Development of Judo in Britain, p.91

Westmorland style of wrestling, and weighing some three stone heavier than the five-foot Japanese, threw his adversary by some trick, not readily to be determined, from the centre of the mat into a pile of chairs stacked up in one corner."[46]

Longhurst never ran his own *dōjō but was a life-long contributor to* jūjutsu, wrestling and self-defence and wrote many books as well as magazine and newspaper articles on the subject.

William Ewart Fairbairn (1885–1960), studied jūjutsu in Shanghai under Professor Okada, who was once the personal instructor to the Emperor of Japan.[47] Fairbairn went on to develop the close-quarter combat method known as 'Defendu'. He trained British commando forces in WWII and he is reputed to have had over 600 encounters outside of training which he distilled into his simple modular combat system.

Image 2 - William Fairbairn [left] (c1940)

---

[46] Longhurst, (1939), *Jiu-Jitsu and other methods of Self-Defence*, p.7
[47] Moclair, (2009), *Ju-Jutsu – A Comprehensive Guide*, p.4

William Bankier (1870–1949) was a generalist strength trainer, boxer, professional wrestler and circus performer working under the stage name of 'Appollo – The Scottish Hercules'.

Image 3 – William Bankier & Yukio Tani (c1905)

Bankier was introduced to Tani by Barton-Wright during one of his music hall demonstration fights and writes of his personal wrestling experience; *"...as he only stands about 5ft in height, it may be easily imagined that the task set before me seemed a particularly light one. To my astonishment, however, he had me at his mercy in less than two minutes. How it was accomplished I did not know, but I lay there at the end of the bout, completely tied up with the Jap laying alongside, grinning from ear to ear and laughingly asking me if I had had enough".* [48]

A small number of Japanese jūjutsu fighters toured British music halls taking on all comers for money. This included Tani, his brother and a Japanese *jūjutsuka* called Sadakazu Uyenishi (1880–c1940), also from Tenjin Shin'yō ryū, whose father, KIchibe Uyenishi, was a *samurai*. Uyenishi's ring name was 'Raku.'

---

[48] Bankier, (1905), *Ju-Jitsu, What it Really Is*, p.25

Image 4 – Yukio Tani (1914)[49]

Image 5 – Sadakazu Uyenishi & Percy Longhurst (1907)[50]

---

[49] Garrud, (1914), *The Complete Jujitsuan*
[50] Uyenishi, (1907), *The Textbook of Ju-Jutsu as Practised in Japan*, p.66

A long list of British challengers ensued keen to prove their strength over the smaller and lighter Japanese adversaries. Bankier, organising some of these contests, speaks of his experience at the time.

"In every place we visited he [Tani] *was a success, taking on all comers, and never failing to defeat his man within the stipulated time of fifteen minutes. Sums have been offered of £20 to any man whom he fails to defeat in the time, and £100 to any man who beats him. In a tour extending over six months, he has defeated on average twenty men each week, and in every case each competitor has been fully two to three, and in many cases six stones heavier than himself."*[51]

Bankier stated that Tani fought under rules where striking was not permitted. The conditions of such a fight would lead Tani to apply his technique unrestrained and lead to unacceptable injury to either man.

Like Tani, to Uyenishi also, the weight of his opponents was a matter of indifference. Needless to say, the challengers were left in admiration of this new fighting style. Uyenishi went on to teach the British military at the Army gymnastic headquarters in Aldershot.

Bankier described Tani's contests in his 1905 book; *"I presume no one will deny Yukio Tani's claim to pre-eminence. Not only in his own style has he excelled. Men of high degree in English methods have fallen prey to him. Their defeat has been most complete and decisive. Tani's triumph is just as simple as his opponent cares to make it. One blow, ever so light on the carpet and the little Jap releases his hold without the slightest ceremony."*[52]

Despite the prizefighting and music hall tours, jūjutsu was not immediately taken up in Britian. Bankier writes in his 1905 account that *"It must be confessed that Ju-Jitsu has completely outlived the dislike of many authorities, who, when Tani, with a fellow-countryman, appeared at the Tivoli, described the science as farcical, and the demonstrator's knockabout comedians."*[53] Jūjutsu's effectiveness was not yet proven to a widespread audience. William Barton-Wright's London based Bartitsu Academy of Physical Culture closed in 1903.

---

[51] Bankier, (1905), *Ju-Jitsu, What it Really Is*, p.28
[52] Bankier, (1905), *Ju-Jitsu, What it Really Is*, p.10
[53] Bankier, (1905), *Ju-Jitsu, What it Really Is*, p.5

Yukio Tani and Sadukazu Uyenishi opened the Japanese School of jūjutsu in London in 1904, based at 305 Oxford Street. By Edwardian jūjutsu had captured the imagination of Britain.

"The ways and means of anticipating attacks are so varied and create such astonishing and marvelously quick results that we in England have long since become alive to the necessity for cultivating the art of Ju-Jitsu. In the army, navy, auxiliary forces, departments of police, schools, colleges and athletic clubs, Tani's system is in vogue."[54]

Jūjutsu began to spread outside of London and training halls started to appear all over the country. Gunju Koizumi (1885-1965) joined the Ashikaga School of Jiu Jitsu in Liverpool (ran by Mr Kara S Ashikaga[55]) after arriving in Prestatyn in 1906. However, it seems that the school closed after a short time (some sources have questioned whether it even existed). Koizumi travelled to London in 1906 to train at both Tani and Uyenishi's dōjōs, before leaving for the USA for a three-year visit in 1907.

Image 6 - Gunju Koizumi (c1906)

"It would be impossible to estimate how many persons learnt jiu jitsu during the period from 1890 to 1911 ... Undoubtedly, Tani and his peers awarded 'Black Sashes' to their most diligent pupils."[56]

---

[54] Bankier, (1905), *Ju-Jitsu, What it Really Is*, p.6
[55] Shortt, (1979), *Beginning Jiu Jitsu Ryoi-Shinto Style*, p.47
[56] Shortt, (1979), *Beginning Jiu Jitsu Ryoi-Shinto Style*, p.49

Around 1910 Bankier introduced Tani to some of his wrestling friends, including Wiliam Garrud, Percy Longhurst, Bruce Sutherland and Percy Bickerdike. This would later lead to the birth of the British Ju Jitsu Society (BJJS) in 1924. All four men became personal students of Tani."[57]

Image 7 – William Garrud (1914)[58]

After World War I, jūjutsu teachers were entering the second or third generation from the first Japanese to teach in the UK (or direct to UK citizens in Japan). These new British instructors formed the first formalised *gaijin goshin* (foreigner's self-defence) jūjutsu syllabuses to begin the process of teaching jūjutsu to the next generation.

In 1918 the (London) Budokwai dōjō was opened by Gunji Koizumi, with Yukio Tani being the chief instructor. Its British founders, E.J. Harrison and W.E. Steers, returned from Japan post World War I after being the first British to be graded as *shodan* in Kōdōkan jūdō in 1913. Fairhurst (1991) described Harrison as the first *gaijin* (foreign) student of Tenshin Shin'yō ryū in Japan.[59]

Glossop, who trained at the Kōdōkan for six months in 1903 quotes Jigorō Kanō as saying: "*You are the second European who has been in our college* [Harrison being the first]. *You are, of course, a friend of Japan, a war correspondent in our midst,*

---

[57] Ross, (2005), *JuJitsu: The Essentials*, p.12
[58] Garrud, (1914), *The Complete Jujitsuan*
[59] Fairhurst, (1991), *Ju Jutsu – The Science The Art*, p.13

and you will consider yourself a guest during lesson hours. Of course your lessons are given gratuitously".[60]

Harrison and Steers *"Both campaigned consistently on behalf of Kodokan judo in preference to jiu jitsu or Ryugi Jiu-do as they called it."*[61] At this time jūdō, ju-ido, and jūjutsu were often considered to be the same thing.

In 1920 Jigorō Kanō was visiting London as a member of the International Olympic Committee and aligned himself to the Budokwai. Tani and Koizumi converted from their jūjutsu styles and aligned their future teachings to Kōdōkan jūdō. Kanō promoting them both to *Nidan* (2ⁿᵈ *dan*) in Kōdōkan jūdō. The ease of transition for Tani and Koizumi from jūjutsu to jūdō is because Kanō's jūdō was based on Kito ryū and Tenjin Shin'yō ryū jūjutsu which they were both familiar with. The older jūjutsu style was therefore only taught to *"a handful of Englishmen who had received the 'black sash' from the likes of Tani and Uyenishi in those early, heady days."*[62]. By 1920 British jūjutsu and jūdō had found their own separate paths.

Table 9 - British jūjutsu and jūdō styles in the early 1900's

Period	British Styles	Influences
1899 - 1918	Jūjutsu	Presence of Japanese jūjutsu instructors coming to Britian
1918 - 1920	Transition phase between jūjutsu only and the introduction of Kodokan Jūdō	The Budokwai and Kano's visit to the UK
1920 Onwards	Jūjutsu Jūdō	Distinct styles and affiliations

Clark (1988) writes of the four Japanese jūjutsu pioneers to the UK: Tani, Uyenishi, Miyake and Koizumi.

"Sada Uyenishi wrote an English language book on jiu jitsu, and trained with Tani. Taru Miyake arrived later and defeated Tani in a contest. For a time, both Tani and Miyake taught at the Oxford St club [Japanese School of Jujitsu]. *Gunji Koizumi*

---

[60] Glossop (1907), *Sunshine and Battlesmoke*, p.64
[61] Shortt, (1979), *Beginning Jiu Jitsu Ryoi-Shinto Style*, p.51
[62] Fairhurst, (1991), *Ju Jutsu – The Science The Art*, p.20

came to Britain in 1906 and taught members of the armed services. In 1918, he opened the Budokwai and asked Yukio Tani to be its chief instructor."[63]

Image 8 – Taro Miyake (c1920)

Table 10 –Japanese jūjutsu instructors in Britain before World War II

Japanese Instructor	Born	In Britain	Parent Martial Art	Publications
Yukio Tani	1881	1900-1950	Fusen ryū, Kodokan jūdō	(1906) The Game of Ju Jitsu
Sadakazu Uyenishi	1880	1900-1907	Tenjin Shinyo ryū, Daito ryū	(1905) The Textbook of Ju-jutsu as Practiced in Japan
Mitsuyo Maeda	1878	1907-1908	Sumō, Tenjin Shin'yo ryū, Kodokan jūdō	-
Taro Miyake	1881	1904-1908	Fusen ryū	(1906) The Game of Ju Jitsu
Gunji Koizumi	1885	1906-1965	Tenjin Shin'yo ryū, Kodokan jūdō	(1960) My Study of Judo: The Principle and the Technical Fundamentals

---

[63] Clark, (1988), Masters' *Jiu Jitsu*, p.19

The question of 'who trained with, and by, who' is summarized in Table 11. Entries marked with a * are unverified during the author's research.

Table 11 – British jūjutsu schools, instructors and members pre-World War II

Baritsu School of Arms and Physical Culture	The School of Japanese Self Defence	Japanese School of Jujitsu	Anglo-Japanese Institute of Self Defence
Shaftsbury Avenue	31 Golden Square, Piccadilly Circus	305 Oxford Street	3 Vernon Place, Bloomsbury Square
London	London	London	London
1900 - 1903	1903 - 1925	1904 - 1906	1905
Edward William Barton-Wright	Sadakazu Uyenishi	Yukio Tani	Sadakazu Uyenishi
Willian Garrud	Willian Garrud	Taru Miyake	Vernon Smith
Edith Garrud	Edith Garrud	Mitsuyo Maeda	
	Percy Longhurst*	Percy Longhurst	
	Gunji Koizumi	W Bruce Sutherland*	
	William E Steers	W. H. Collingridge[64]	
	W Bruce Sutherland*	Percy Bickerdike*	
	Percy Bickerdike*		
	Phoebe Roberts		
	Emily Watts[65]		
	Jack Britten*		

---

[64] Collingridge, (1915), *Tricks of Self-Defence*
[65] Watts, (1906), *The Fine Art of Jujitsu*, p.1

University of Cambridge	Kara Ashikaga School of Jujutsu	Army Gymnastic Headquarters	The Budokwai
Trinity Lane	4 Electric Buildings, Maryland Street	Queen's Avenue	Lower Grosvenor Place
Cambridge	Liverpool	Aldershot	London
1906 - Present	1906 - 1906	c1908 - c1939	1918 - Present
Yukio Tani	Gunji Koizumi	Sadakazu Uyenishi	Gunji Koizumi
Gunji Koizumi		Captain Leopold McLaglan[66]	Yukio Tani
Mitsuyo Maeda			William E Steers
Mikinosuke Kawaishi			Earnest Harrison
			Jigoro Kano
			William Bankier
			Trevor Pryce Leggett

The Alpha School of Ju-Jitsu	British Ju Jitsu Society Members	Skyner's Ju-Jitsu
Kensington area	-	Mount Pleasant & Catherine Street
Liverpool	Britain	Liverpool
1924	1924	1928
Jack Britten	William Bankier	Mikonosuke Kawaishi
Robert Clark	Percy Bickerdike	Gerald Skyner
	Percy Longhurst	
	W Bruce Sutherland	
	Harry H Hunter*	

---

[66] McLaglan, (1922), *Police Jiu Jitsu*

Image 9 – Tani and Miyake's Japanese School of Ju Jitsu (1906)[67]

Emily Watts trained with Uyenishi and wrote 'The Fine Art of Jujutsu' in 1906 as an instruction method to other students, Uyenishi was used as an *uke* in some of the photographs for the more difficult throws. The other photos are Watt's female students throwing her. Jūjitsu at the time was being taught to women as well as men, Edith Garrud (1872–1971) instructed with her husband William at the Golden Square dojo after Unyeshi left Britain to travel Europe in 1907. Notably Edith is also famous for training the suffragette movement in self-defence. Emily and Edith were some of the first female martial arts instructors in the Western world.

Image 10 - Emily Watts throwing Uyenishi with a tomonage throw[68]

---

[67] Tani & Miyake, (1906), *The Game of Ju Jitsu*
[68] Watts (1906), *The Fine Art of Jujutsu*, p.141

Image 11 - Edith Garrud Demonstrating Jujutsu for the Suffragette movement

The first instructors of the British Ju Jitsu Society (BJJS) were participants who were awarded the 'Black Sashes' from Tani and Uyenishi between 1904 and 1918. The BJJS did not become Budokwai affiliates and the Budokwai did not recognise them.

After the formation of the Budokwai in 1918, a myriad of other jūdō, jūjutsu and jiu-do clubs and associations were established throughout Britain. Some were aligned with the Budokwai, with others joining the British Ju Jitsu Society (BJJS) (formed in 1924) and still others, going it alone. Rules, regulations and grading standards differed from one school to another.

British jūdo and jūjutsu styles were going on their separate paths. The British Ju Jitsu Society (BJJS) formed strong links with the British Amateur Wrestling Association, with Percy Longhurst belonging to both organisations.

In Liverpool, Harry H Hunter and Jack Britten were teaching jūjutsu. Hunter claimed to be the 'Ju-Jitsu champion Europe' and trained many police forces.[69]

---

[69] Hunter, (1927), *Super Ju-Jitsu*

Image 12 - Harry H Hunter[70]

Jack Britten, a London-born boxer, having served in the trenches of World War I is thought to have studied under Tani and Uyenishi (between 1904 and 1914) although there are no definitive records to support this. Britten set up the Alpha Ju Jitsu school in Liverpool in 1921. The school focused on a more jūjutsu style and approach as opposed to the Budokwai, who were teaching Kōdōkan jūdō style. Around the same time, Ernie Hurrell was teaching jūjutsu style in Chester. His style was reputed to be 'brutal.'

Image 13 – Jack Britten (c1921)[71]

---

[70] Hunter, (1927), *Super Ju-Jitsu*, p.8
[71] Breen, (2012), *A History of Ju-Jitsu*.

The third Liverpool based school of jūjutsu (behind Koizumi's Ashikaga school and Britton's Alpha school) was Skyner's jūjutsu school formed in 1928 by Gerald Skyner, an ex-army combat instructor and student of Mikonosuke Kawaishi.[72]

Image 14 - Gerald Skyner (c1928)

Image 15 - Mikonosuke Kawaishi

I. Kimura and S. Yoshima (5th *dans* in Yoshin ryū) came to Britain in 1933 under invitation from the British Ju Jitsu Society (BJJS) and began teaching jūjutsu in Bournemouth. Two 4th *dans* joined them in 1934, H. Kawamura and M. Kobayashi.

---

[72] Keegan, (2010), *British Jujutsu.*

Before the outbreak of World War II, the four Yoshin ryū masters, Kimura, Yoshima, Kawamura and Kobayashi graded seven Englishmen.[73]

Post World War II

The British Ju Jitsu Society (BJJS) lost nearly all of its Japanese instructors due to the outbreak of World War II. Ironically, at the time, the two countries with the strongest links to British jūjutsu were Germany and Japan.

Shortt (1979) describes the renaissance of British jūjutsu after World War II: *"Teppei Seika was invited to teach Tenjin Shin'yo Ryu to members of the Kano Jiu Jitsu Society... later became the British Ju-Jutsu Federation in 1956. In Liverpool the British Ju-Jitsu Association which had been founded in that city before the war was re-started by James Blundell ... In Bournemouth, one of the surviving Yoshin Ryu members, Kenneth Dunn-Hardiman restarted the school of Yoshin Ryu that had started before the war broke out."*[74]

"James Blundell originally studied jiu jitsu under Harry H. Hunter and his assistant William Green. Robert Clark studied under the late Jack Britten."[75]

Image 16 – Robert Clark (c1979)[76]

---

[73] Shortt, (1979), *Beginning Jiu Jitsu Ryōi-Shinto Style*, p.56
[74] Shortt, (1979), *Beginning Jiu Jitsu Ryōi-Shinto Style*, p.65
[75] Shortt, (1979), *Beginning Jiu Jitsu Ryōi-Shinto Style*, p.133
[76] Breen, (2012), *A History of Ju-Jitsu*.

Robert Clark (1946–2012) left Jack Britton's Alpha Jiu Jitsu club at some point in the 1960's to train under James Blundell (1921–1989) at the Liverpool BJJA.[77]

Image 17 – James Blundell (c1960)

In 1956 the Liverpool based British Ju Jitsu Association (BJJA) was formed by James Blundell, his organised and methodical jūjutsu syllabus influenced by the (1905) *Textbook of Ju-Jutsu as Practiced in Japan* by Uyenishi.[78]

In 1968 the British Ju Jutsu Federation (BJJF) merged with the Nakama No Ju Jitsu (NNJJ) to form the British Isles Ju Jitsu Federation (BIJJF).

In 1970 the Liverpool BJJA formalised a tie with the Jiu Jitsu Black Belt Federation of America (JJBBFA)[79] leading to the 1976 formation of the World Jiu Jitsu Federation (WJJF) of which the BJJA was a branch. The WJJF had, by 1979, 44 member countries.[80] Blundell, Clark and Morris developed the syllabus for the WJJA. Blundell was the founder and figurehead, Clark was the chief instructor and Morris the chairman.[81]

In 1974 the British Ju Jitsu Board of Control (BJJBC) was set up with the aid of the governmental 'Sports Council' and the 'Central Council for Physical Recreation.' In 1975 the BIJJF was dissolved. The BJJA then joined the BJJBC to work towards a

---

[77] Brough, (2018), *The History of Bushido & British Ju Jitsu*.

[78] Keegan, (2019), *Bushido – A complete History of British JuJutsu*, p.95

[79] Shortt, (1979), *Beginning Jiu Jitsu Ryoi-Shinto Style*, p.66

[80] Clark, (1979), *World Ju Jitsu Federation Program*, p.4

[81] Brough, (2018), *The History of Bushido & British Ju Jitsu*.

single governing body for British jūjutsu. In 1976 the Liverpool-based BJJA and the BJJBC merged to reconstitute as the (new) BJJA.

After a period of growth, the British government became concerned about the standards of martial arts teaching and regulation and, in 1977 formed the Martial Arts Commission (MAC). This was designed to regulate the other individual and varying regulatory bodies for all martial arts practiced in Britain. Individual associations were invited to apply to be accepted and recognised by the MAC.

The MAC brought together the newly formed BJJA with its founding members including James Blundell, Robert Clark and Richard Morris, themselves now two generations away from the first Japanese to teach in Britain.

Clark states in 1988: *"...responsible members of Britain's martial arts community enlisted the aid of the Sports Council, the Home Office and the Department of the Environment in setting up a recognised umbrella controlling body which would identify safe, competent martial art. That body is the Martial Arts Commission (M.A.C)."*[82] Registration to the MAC was sporadic with some clubs choosing to align and merge themselves whilst others chose to go it alone.

The BJJA and WJJF split in the 1980s, Clark staying with the WJJF and Blundell the BJJA. Morris resigned from both appointments in 1986 to found Jiu Jitsu International (JJI).[83] At this point British jūjutsu had splintered and central control for the majority of different associations under a single governing body was all but lost. The BJJA had official control under British government, but many clubs went their own way, and continue to do so.

In 1988 the BJJA was reconstituted to include other affiliated Ju-Jitsu associations.[84] The MAC was disbanded by the UK government in 1991 and responsibility was taken over by the 'Sports Council' (itself founded in 1972). In 1993 the BJJA became the British Ju-Jitsu Association Governing Body (BJJA GB)[85] led by Martin Dixon.

---

[82] Clark, (1988), *Masters Jiu Jitsu*, p.116
[83] London JuJutsu, *Richard Morris 10th Dan*.
[84] BJJA GB, (2019), *About the BJJA GB*.
[85] BJJA GB, (2019), *About the BJJA GB*.

In 1994 the Sports Council made the decision to rename itself the 'UK Sports Council' and to move away from its policy of 'sport for all' in order to concentrate on funding only those sports in which the UK could succeed on the world stage.

Mass participation was now overseen by local authorities. The UK Sports Council was renamed again in 1997 to 'UK Sport' who were now also responsible for distributing lottery funding. UK Sport honed its funding down further to elite sport and established a closer relationship with the International Olympic Association. Within UK Sport, individual nations are represented by; Sport England, Sport Scotland, Sport Wales and Sport Northern Ireland.

Today UK Sport recognises the British Ju-Jitsu Association GB (BJJA GB) as the governmental representative for British jūjutsu. However, today in Britain, just as in ancient Japan, many independent schools exist with their own syllabuses, rules, and variations. A similar problem was incurred in Japan in 1906 when 14 contemporary jūjutsu schools (including the Kōdōkan) met to standardise jūjutsu kata.

Internationally there is no standardised syllabus or rank recognition in jūjutsu and no internationally recognised format for competition or rules currently exists. There is a lot of variation and specialisation from a myriad of different clubs and associations. Mol (2001) sums up this problem by highlighting that a *"lack of standardisation has meant that jujutsu has now been changed into something that it was never meant to be."*[86]

Brazilian Jiu Jitsu

BJJ was largely unheard of until its explosive demonstration at UFC 1 in 1993. Unlike traditional Jiu Jitsu BJJ came first to America, and then to the UK in the late 1990's. *"Mauricio Gomes and Chen Moraes started teaching at the Custard Factory in Birmingham and the Budokwai in London."*[87] The first BJJ seminar in the UK was by Arlans Sequeria in Tottenham in 1997. Moraes in 1998 and Gomes in 1998. The first British BJJ tournament was run by Chen Moraes in 1999.

In 2021 the UKBJJA became the official national governing body for Brazilian Jiu Jitsu in the UK.

---

[86] Mol, (2001), *Classic Fighting Arts of Japan*, p.222
[87] UKBJJA.org/about

The History of American Jūjutsu

The earliest days of American jūjutsu, (as they are for other countries) follow a largely similar path to that of Britain whereby the pioneers of the art were stationed in the Westernising Japan for work, police or military reasons and learned the art there bringing it (and some of its Japanese proponents) back home with them.

Jigorō Kanō sent Yamashita Yoshaiki to the USA in 1889 to teach jūdō at Harvard and Annapolis. Yamashita went on to found the first jūdō dōjō in Seattle in 1903.

Records of the next jūdō dōjō is the Shunyokan Judo Club in Hawaii, founded by Shigemi Teshima and Naomatsu Kaneshige in 1913.

The *"Fathers of American Jujitsu were not even American. Both were British. John J. O'Brien… The second "Brit," William Fairbairn"*.[88] Jūjutsu as recognisable in modern America was largely initiated by these two early pioneers.

Image 18 – John O'Brien (c1905)

O'Brien (1880–1938) arrived in San Francisco in 1900. Much like William Bankier did with Tani and Unyeshi in the British music halls, O'Brien began touring jūjutsu through the USA via circuses and vaudeville acts.

---

[88] Sainthilaire, (2021), *Pioneers of American JuJitsu*, p11

O'Brien introduced President Theodore Roosevelt to jujutsu who took lessons from him at the Whitehouse, Roosevelt also later also studied jūdō. O'Brien was inducted into the U.S. Army at the beginning of WWI and became a hand-to-hand combat instructor. Teaching other Captain's such as Allan Corstorphin Smith.

Corstorphin Smith (c1890-1962) was born in Scotland and received his Shodan in jūdō at the Kōdōkan in 1916. After training in jūjutsu with O'Brien he went on to further develop military fighting techniques and publish a 1920 book entitled: *the secrets of Jujitsu*.

We know of Fairbairn's exploits in Shanghai and training of British commandos in WWII. His self-defence manual *All in Fighting* was published as *Get Tough* in the USA. Fairbairn was requested, during WWII to come to America and train his '*Defendu*' style to U.S. soldiers and special forces. Fairbairn stayed in the US until the end of WWII, his relationship with the British, Canadian and American military continued well into his retirement where he continued to work as a consultant.

Irving Hancock (1868-1922) wrote several books on jūjutsu and studied in New York City teaching a Tsutsumi ryū style.

By 1905 Yamashita Yoshaiki was hired as jūdō coach for the U.S. Naval Academy.

Tomita Tsunejirō and Mitsuyo Maeda had demonstrated jūjutsu at the West Point military academy, also in 1905 but the contract was awarded to Tom Jenkins a world champion professional wrestler.

Tengan Uchimura is a less well known Japanese *jūjutsuka* teaching Tenjin Shin'yō ryū style in Cambridge Massachusetts around 1905. Uchimura started what was possibly the first jujutsu school in America[89].

In c1905 Mitsuyo Maeda started a jujutsu school at 190 High Street in Brooklyn. The school was presumably unsuccessful as Maeda moved to Britain in 1907 and later to Cuba before moving to Brazil in 1914, eventually he took on Carlos Gracie as a student which lead to the creation of Brazilian Jiu Jitsu and the explosion in popularity of mixed martial arts contests.

Taro Miyake moved from Britain to Seattle in 1914 where he settled for 20yrs.

---

[89] Shaw (2022), *https://www.youtube.com/watch?v=az7DzL7B_YE*

Henry S. Okazaki (1890-1951) Moved to Hawaii in 1908 bringing his Daido Ryū style to the island. Okazaki later called his style Kodenkan jiu jitsu in honour of Kano's Kōdōkan judo. Later Okazaki started teaching Danzan ryū style. Okazaki was one of the first Japanese practitioners to teach Jūjutsu to Americans in America, this was virtually unheard of before then.

Wally Jay (1917-2011) began training Danzan ryū Jūjutsu from a student of Osazaki, Juan Gomez in 1940. Wally Jay went on to found Small Circle Ju Jitsu and exchange teachings with other martial arts pioneers, including Bruce Lee.

Osazaki founded the American Jiu-Jitsu Institute in 1943.

Brazilian Jiu Jitsu

After earlier visits from Rolls Gracie in the 1960's and Carley Gracie in 1972. Rorion Gracie came to America in 1978 and started teaching Brazilian Jiu Jitsu from his garage in Hermosa beach California. The garage had become too busy for Rorion to run on his own so in 1985 his 18yr old brother Royce Gracie came to California to help run the classes.

By 1989 another of Rorion's brothers Rickson Gracie and his cousin Rigan Machado had moved to California to support Rorion in the opening of the 'Gracie Academy' in Torrance.

Richard Bresler was the first American student [90] and Craig Kukkuk the first American blackbelt of BJJ.

Image 19 – Rickson, Royce and Rigan at the Gracie Academy (c1989)

[90] Bresler, (2021), *Worth Defending*

After a couple of years Rickson Gracie and Rigan Machado left the Gracie Academy. Rickson Gracie and the Machado brothers John, Carlos and Jean Jacques left setup their own gyms. As Rorion had trademarked the 'Gracie Jiu Jitsu' name, other members of the family had to call their art 'Brazilian Jiu Jitsu', this is how the art would be referred to from that point onwards[91].

In 1986 Carlos Gracie Jr (1956) setup the first 'Gracie Barra' school in Barra da Tijuca, Rio de Janeiro Brazil. Today Gracie Barra is the most expansive BJJ organisation in the world, the headquarters moved to Lake Forest USA.

It took Rorion until the launch of the Ultimate Fighting Championship, (UFC) with Art Davie in 1993 for BJJ to go mainstream. Royce Gracie was the smallest and lightest competitor on the roster and won convincingly against all the other martial artists.

Carlos Gracie Jr setup the International Brazilian Jiu Jitsu Federation (IBJJF) in 1994 to regulate the art of BJJ and competitions.

In 2000 an American athlete, BJ Penn won the Word Jiu Jitsu Championship in Brazil. BJ Penn would go on the break records in MMA by becoming the first athlete to win belts in two different weight classes.

---

[91]Rickson Gracie (2021), *Breathe*

Classical, Traditional and Modern Jūjutsu

Table 12 – Four main (historical) classifications of jūjutsu

Early Classical Jūjutsu	Ancient styles of Japanese *bujutsu*	(794–1606)	Japanese *Koryū* Martial Arts
Late Classical Jūjutsu	*Budō* styles, such as Takenouchi ryū, Yoshin ryū and Ryoi Shinto ryū	(1603-1868)	
Traditional Jūjutsu	Systems derived after the Meiji restoration from late classical jūjutsu with modern influences	(1868-1926)	Japanese *Gendai* Martial Arts
Modern Jūjutsu	Traditional jūjutsu developed by non-Japanese	(1926-Present)	

1. Early Classical Jūjutsu

Also referred to as: **Yawara | *Koryū* jūjutsu**

From the Heian (794–1185) to the Azuchi-Momoyama (1568–1603) period. Life-or-death *bujutsu* training for the full time warrior.

Techniques based primarily on opponents wearing armour.

2. Late Classical Jūjutsu

Also referred to as: **Jūjutsu proper | Edo jūjutsu |*Koryū* jūjutsu**

Budō styles, such as Takenouchi ryū, Yoshin ryū and Ryoi Shinto ryū.

Through the Edo / Tokugawa (1603–1868) period.

"Today, most of the Koryu jujitsu (old schools of jujitsu) are practically extinct or only practiced in family clans or in small study groups. With the advent of modern martial arts, or Gendai Budo, throughout the twentieth century the Koryu have lost the interest and influence that made them great in the past."[92]

The 'golden age' of jūjutsu where hand-to-hand, non-armoured techniques (including striking) were refined and developed.

---

[92] Caracena, (2017), *Tenjin Shinyo Ryu JuJutsu*, p.11

3. Traditional Jūjutsu
Also referred to as: *Nihon goshin* jūjutsu | *Gendai* jūjutsu
Systems derived from classical jūjutsu with modern influences.
From the Meiji (1868–1912) to the Taishō (1912–1926) period.

"Years of peace, societal transformation, Westernisation, and the adoption of modern methods of warfare made it clear that for the more enlightened samurai (among others), survival and growth rested on transformation, acceptance, innovation and change. The message was clear. Adapt or fade away into obscurity."[93]

4. Modern Jūjutsu
Also referred to as: *Gaijin goshin* jūjutsu | *Gendai* jujutsu | *Gendai Būdo*
Traditional jūjutsu developed by non-Japanese.
From the Shōwa (1926–1989) period to the present day.

Modern jūjutsu focused on self-defence or competition as well as character building and personal development.

Often jūjutsu schools term themselves as 'traditional', 'classical' or 'Japanese' to differentiate themselves from jūdō or Brazilian jiu jitsu. In reality, these schools based outside Japan are most probably teaching *gaijin goshin* jūjutsu (foreigners self-defence jūjutsu).

Modern Classifications of Jūjutsu
The use of unarmed combat (including jūjutsu) can be largely divided into three categories as shown in Table 13.

Table 13 – Modern categorisations of unarmed combat usage

Those who defend the country against foreigners	Military
Those who defend the country from its citizens	Police
Those who defend themselves from other citizens	General public

Twenty-first century developments have led to a clouding of these three distinct categories but in principle the military need to kill (or capture by any means

---

[93] Yiannakis, (2017), *Jujutsu – Traditions, Ways & Modern Practices*, p.10

necessary) their opponents, the police to restrain and capture without harm to the assailant and the public need to defend to enable an escape.

Goshin Jūjutsu

The Japanese kanji for goshin 護身 means self-protection or self-defence. 護 being to protect or safeguard and 身 being body or self.

Goshin jūjutsu is not necessarily a battlefield syllabus. Moreover, techniques are updated through the lessons of actual experience of violent encounter, muggings, assault, security and police work. Killing is rarely necessary even though it may be the intent of the adversary. Techniques are biased towards immobilising or incapacitating the opponent.

"Many of the modern Ju-Jutsu schools would be better classified as Goshin Jutsu or Self Defence systems which are simplified versions of the older more complex systems ... The modern Goshin systems can often be quite small in content allowing the practitioner to gain a degree of expertise and ability within a reasonable time period ... ."[94]

Tatsu Tanaka started his school of *goshin* Jiu Jutsu in Tokyo in 1952. Taking inspiration from Kanō's jūdō, he stripped back the school's syllabus to around 150 basic techniques considered for his modern students. *"Tanaka promptly set to work screening out the safe, practical tactics from his own Yagyu-Shingan-Ryū and from two other jujitsu schools."*[95]

Modern *goshin* jūjutsu students are not full-time warriors with full battlefield strategy and prowess over all available weaponry and techniques. *Goshin* jūjutsu is a simplified version of the older more classical systems. It is notable that the further back in time one travels, the more simplified the system becomes before new expertise was added. Modern *goshin* systems allow the student to progress in a reasonable amount of time with a level of expertise commensurate with effective self-defence in modern society.

---

[94] Davies, (1989), *Traditional and Modern Ju-Jitsu*, p.11
[95] Adams, (1968), *Black Belt Magazine*, p.13

Combat Jūjutsu

The Japanese kanji for jissen 実践 means real combat or combat reality. 実 being reality or truth and 践 being combat.

Jūjutsu started as a battlefield art, secondary to a warrior's primary weapon but still very much used for life-and-death struggle. *"From the late 17th century to the middle of the 19th century, combat ju-jutsu was widely practiced by the samurai. In peace time, however the ju-jutsu lost its emphasis on combat."*[96]

Jūjutsu was refined in later periods and used in non-lethal competition. In peace time the combat-hardened *samurai* moved to other associated professions with some becoming bone setters as they were used to having to deal with frequent injuries. Other, now unemployed *samurai* used their skills to put on wrestling shows or become bouncers or gangsters. Later, the banned *samurai* taught some of the arts to commoners. Ultimately, techniques entered the *ryū* that would be seen as unnecessary or ineffective in real life-and-death combat.

On the battlefield a *samurai* encounter had three possible outcomes:

1. The death of the *samurai*
2. The death of his opponent
3. A mutual slaying

There was no room for showmanship or ineffective technique with two out of three scenarios carrying the risk of death. The incentive to develop simple, effective technique is obvious.

In today's society, these techniques are understandably of great interest to modern-day military and specialised security agencies. The spirit and intent with which they are practiced in these situations cannot be fully replicated in the *dōjō* and can come only from actual combat experience.

The techniques used in combat jūjutsu must evolve from actual life-or-death experience, or they will have no validity when put to the test. In some ways,

---

[96] Rahming, (1991), *Combat Ju-Jutsu*, p.17

combat jūjutsu, as it is practiced today, militarily has returned full circle to the (pre-Edo / Tokugawa) **Early Classical** jūjutsu of the *samurai*.

Taiho Jitsu

The Japanese kanji for taiho 逮捕 means police or arrest techniques. 逮 being apprehend or chase and 捕 being catch or capture.

Around 1920 the *Keishichō* (Tokyō police) developed a separate arm of their jūdō training for their elite police force. As jūdō had almost eliminated the use of striking (except in *kata* format) the Tokyō police force reorganised some of these techniques into their *taiho* jūjutsu syllabus.

In 1931 Shimizu Takaji assisted in forming the Tokubetsu Keibitai (Japanese special police), Takaji's keijo-jutsu survived the 1945 ban on martial arts in Japan as it was required to be taught to all policemen.

Brazilian Jiu Jitsu (BJJ)

Brazilian Jiu Jitsu is a dedicated set of ne-waza techniques based on the jūdō taught in Brazil at the time. The Japanese kanji for ne-waza is 寝技,寝業. 寝 being to lie down, 技 for skill or art and 業 for vocation or performance.

More information on BJJ can be found on page 128. Brazilian Jiu Jitsu can be further divided in four sub-sections as shown in Table 14.

Table 14 – Sub-sections of Brazilian Jiu Jitsu

Gi
No *Gi*
MMA
Self-Defence

There are other modern classifications of jūjutsu with more being added all the time, these four (goshin, combat, taiho and Brazilian) would cover a large sample of what we know today being taught as jūjutsu.

The Future of Jūjutsu

Just as the ancient *samurai* of Japan adapted their techniques to the changes of battlefield technology and shifts in society, so modern day jūjutsu follows a similar path. Criminals, muggers, hooligans and rapists have changed little over time and so jūjutsu can still be effective as protection from these threats if other means are not immediately available.

Traditional jūjutsu techniques are still taught and learned by many, but increasingly the art is being diluted and cross-contaminated with new techniques favoring the old. Jūjutsu has survived 1,500 years of clan warfare, the rise and fall of *shōguns*, removal and loss of ancient *makimono*, the modernisation of a closed society, and world globalisation.

As Clark (1988) summarized, *"Jiu jitsu has not stopped developing. New applications of technique constantly add to the syllabus. That is why the art itself will never become obsolete."*[97]

A growing number of clubs are taking the principles of jūjutsu and melding other complementary techniques into their syllabus to keep pace with society and modern military applications. This follows the second rule of self-defence: *"**If it works, use it!**"*[2].

With the popularity of competitive MMA, jūdō and Brazilian jiu jitsu there are a growing number of instructors and competitors who are modern full-time martial artists and cross training between the three branches of jūjutsu, further diluting the distinctions between each art.

This cross-over offers the modern student the benefit of being able to train three arts in one *dōjō* and will, in itself, lead to further cross-contamination, the future distinction of jūjutsu becoming the student's adaptation to the rules of competition whether that be BJJ, jūdō or MMA.

---

[97] Clark, (1988), *Masters' Jiu Jitsu*, p.12

Figure 12 – Cross-Over Between jūjutsu, jūdō and Brazilian jiu jitsu

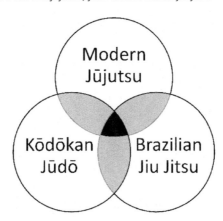

Whichever style of jūjutsu favors the student's personal needs, there is currently enough choice and instruction for everyone to choose their own path. This in itself will provide a natural direction for the future of jūjutsu.

The current popularity of each *ryū* will determine its future teacher-to-student survival.

Chapter 3: Mentality

メンタリティ

Jūjutsu Etiquette

In a modern world where technology affords greater access to resources and shortcuts, most jūjutsu clubs still retain a degree of formality and a formal code of etiquette from the moment a student enters the *dōjō* to when they leave. The club *sensei* decides the degree of formality for their club or session.

Each association, club, *dōjō* and *sensei* will have their own rules, although some of the more common aspects would be accepted worldwide: good manners, a respect for each other and the Japanese culture from which jūjutsu was created.

The Dōjō

The *dōjō* is the place students come to train under the safety and supervision of the *sensei*. Modern *dōjōs* range from purpose-built facilities with permanent *tatami*, down to temporary, multi-functional halls where the *tatami* are laid out and put away for every session. The role of teaching new students about the *dōjō* rules is usually left down to the *senpai* (student leader). The Japanese word for etiquette is *reishiki*.

Common *dōjō* rules may include:

- *Rei* before and after training with your *uke*
- No smoking, drinking or swearing around the *dōjō*
- Good personal hygiene must observed and *gi* must be clean
- Finger and toenails should be cut short and long hair tied back
- No jewelry or watches on the *tatami*
- Gaining permission from the *sensei* before stepping on and off the *tatami*
- Training should not take place under the influence of alcohol or drugs

In the military, respect is observed by a salute, in business by a handshake; in jūjutsu respect for training partners, the training environment and the teacher is shown in the form of a bow. Jūjutsu students (*deshi*) should *rei* (bow) whilst facing the *tatami* on entry and exit to the *dōjō*. The standing *rei* is called *ritsu-rei*.

Tori always bows to *uke* before beginning to train together. The bow is a sign of mutual respect and understanding.

"He who is to do well in the mastery of jiu-jitsu must have from the outset a friend with whom he can practice the work continuously and enthusiastically. This

practice must be had daily, and must be carried on with as much severity as can be employed without inflicting injury of serious nature."[98]

The Tatami

Jūjutsu and jūdō's equivalent of the boxing 'knock out' is to throw the opponent down onto a rubberised mat. In the *dōjō* this does not look very severe, but it must be remembered that *tori* is actively trying to protect *uke* whilst throwing him. *Uke* is trained to fall without injury and the *tatami* is designed to absorb the impact. In a self-defence scenario the aggressor would land awkwardly, with more force, onto a hard surface. It is likely they would be knocked out or incapacitated with one well-executed throw.

The *tatami* in modern jūjutsu consist of a rubberised jūdō mat typically 2m x 1m x 40mm thick. Six modern jūdō mats are an ideal *dōjō* size for two people to practice properly. Traditionally *"The Japanese floor mat called tatami is usually about 6ft long, 3ft wide, and 2in thick, consisting of took (made of rice straw bound together), tightly covered with a straw mat called the omote, with the edges neatly bordered with cloth."*[99]

Formality in the Dōjō

Deshi should face the *kamiza* area of the *dōjō* and *rei* when stepping on and off the *tatami*. Modern *dōjōs* may not have a *kamiza* area, so *deshi* should face the centre of the *tatami* and *rei*.

The *kamiza* area of the *dōjō* is traditionally a place of honour which would be reserved for the most senior *dan* grades. Often this area can contain a picture of the chief instructor of founder.

The kneeling position (sitting on the heels) is called *seiza* and translates as 'proper sitting' in English. In the Muromachi period of Japan (1336-1573), this was considered to be a respectful way to sit. The *samurai* are credited with teaching its widespread use in historical Japan. Today *seiza* is used in the *dōjō* as a formal way of starting and finishing the class.

A traditional class begins in *seiza*, and when the *sensei* has signaled they are ready, the senior student will call *"mokusō"* which is the mediation period to mentally

---

[98] Hancock, (1904), *Jiu-Jitsu Combat Tricks*, p.6
[99] Harrison, (1950), *The Fighting Spirit of Japan*, p.14

prepare for training before the *seiza rei*. *Mockuso* is brought to a halt by the senior student calling *"yame"* (stop).

After *mockusō*, the *sensei* may turn to the *dōjō* shrine and the senior student can call out *"shōmeninrei"* (bow to the teacher) so all can bow in respect. Once the sensei has turned to face his students, the senior student can call out *"onegaishemasu"* (please teach me) after which the full class bows to the *sensei*. The *sensei* returns the bow by bowing lower than his students to signify his humility.

The second most important area of the *dōjō* is called the *jōseki*. This is where the *sensei* can choose to place the *yūdansha* (black belts). Traditionally they would kneel in grade order from the left hand side of the *sensei*.

The *shimoseki* area of the *dōjō* is reserved for lower *dan* grades. The *mudansha* (coloured belt) grades begin training by lining up in the *shimoza* area.

It is common for *jūjutsuka* to perform *zazen* (a seated meditation) in the *seiza* position. This is a more focused and highly concentrated meditation than the earlier aforementioned *mokusō*. The *samurai* believed that the right side was always stronger than the left, therefore all *samurai* were right-handed. When going into *seiza*, the weak side (left) always touches the floor first, and the strong side (right) always rises first.

In a traditional *dōjō*, at the end of the class and before the *sensei* rises from *seiza*, students must present themselves, kneeling, in front of the *sensei* to be recognised and bow deeply to thank the *sensei* for their teaching. After the bow, the student can shuffle backwards on their knees before standing to exit the *tatami*.

Seiza is performed by lowering down on the left knee first, leaving 2 fist-widths between the knees keeping the back straight sitting down onto the heels with palms resting high on the thighs. When standing the right leg always rises first.

Seiza rei is the kneeling bow. *Ritsu rei* is the standing bow.

The Spirit and Philosophy of Jūjutsu

"No matter whether a person belongs to the upper or lower ranks, if he has not put his life on the line at least once he has cause for shame". Nabeshima Naoshige (1538-1611).[100]

Jūjutsu as practiced by the samurai is not a sport, attempts at creating a sport-only based version of jūjutsu can be damaging to its self-defence and pure combat capabilities. The *jutsu* or science of jūjutsu in its original form is a killing and subduing art.

For the ancient Japanese masters, jūjutsu (or, more broadly; *budō*) was a way of life. Modern society has made it difficult to replicate this in its entirety.

A *jūjutsuka* should, over the course of their training, aim to overcome their ego, develop and espouse the values of their *dōjō* and promote the ideals of the art. A side effect of training with the true spirit of the martial arts is to develop the student's tolerance of others, patience, respect and a calm persona.

Jūjutsu has no religious bearing, but it was formed in a time and society where Buddhism, Taoism and Confucianism were prevalent. The *samurai* would have taken many lives in a violent and torturous manner, and morality was more centered around a code of honour than conventional visions of right or wrong.

Jūjutsu is esoteric. That is to say, it is understood by only a small number of people with specialist knowledge. This is not unusual for many of the Japanese martial arts as they were traditionally passed on from teacher to pupil by word of mouth. A person cannot become an instant expert at jūjutsu. It takes many years and requires patience, repetition, and the cooperation of a teacher and fellow students. *"It is a general attitude of the mind at a certain stage, and a very natural attitude too, if one takes the trouble to look into it."*[101]

The 'science of softness' translation of jūjutsu should not be interpreted incorrectly. The softness comes from using minimal force to overcome the opponent which can be very different to the outcome of using that force. Clark (1988) explains *" … if your opponent pulls you, push against him. If he pushes you*

---

[100] Scott Wilson, (1982), *Ideals of the Samurai*, p.118
[101] Hancock, (1950), *The Fighting Spirit of Japan*, p.96

back, pull him after you. Only a small amount of force used in this way, is needed to produce a large response."[102]

The ancient oriental philosophy of jūjutsu is difficult for most people in Western society to emulate. Through jūjutsu training, even haphazardly, the values associated with the art will develop within the student.

Skinner (1904) states that those who practice jūjutsu " ... *do not meet force with force opposing the fierce rush of an enemy or trying to stop a heavy fist with some part of the body. This would be contrary, the gentle artist with his imperturbable smile, instead of trying to obstruct, politely helps his enemy along, to his own undoing.*"[103]

Training in jūjutsu increases self-confidence should a situation requiring self-defence become unavoidable. Anger is a negative emotion that impairs the connection between mind and body, resulting in a loss of technique. A cool demeanor can be less intimidating, but will allow the *jūjutsuka* to appear nonchalant, and channel their training to work to maximum effect.

A fully rounded *jūjutsuka* must have the correct mental attitude paired with the correct physical technique.

"In jiu-jitsu extreme discipline of the mind is both a requirement and a result."[104]

Like most physical activities, constant practice is required to keep the student's technique most effective. Students who do not practice will suffer in speed and skill levels, and the neuromuscular pathways that create 'muscle memory' will become slower without the training 'reminders' given through constant repetition.

"Rapidity is essential to success, but accuracy is even more so. Without complete accuracy – and this includes not only the action of the arms but the movements and placing of the feet and the posture of the body – the effort will be a failure ... Perfection of arm work will be wasted if the feet are improperly placed or a wrong inclination given to the body."[105]

---

[102] Clark (1988), *Masters' Jiu Jitsu*, p.9
[103] Skinner, (1904), *Jiu-Jitsu – The Japanese Method of Attack and Self Defense*.
[104] Hancock, (1904), *Jiu-Jitsu Combat Tricks*, p.151
[105] Garrud, (1947), *The Complete Jujitsuan*, p.xv

Fudo is a *samurai* concept of 'non-movement'. Gluck (1973) credits Monk Takuan with developing and naming the concept. The antagonist generates motion when making an attack and therefore has inertia to overcome when changing direction. *"But the man whose mind and intuition are ever active and are awake and whose physical attitudes are passively ready has no inertia. This becomes the basis of jujutsu and the newly developing Japanese way of the sword, Kendo."*[106]

Fu dō shin is the *samurai* frame of mind and spirit of the warrior, literally translated as 'do as usual with unshakable mind'. The premise of *fu dō shin* is that the task outweighs any personal sacrifice; including one's own death. Clearly this is rather extreme in modern times outside of perhaps a modern soldier's remit. The average *jūjutsuka* should be honoured that the techniques they are using were developed under this extreme focus, from which the modern student can now benefit.

Traditional jūjutsu includes the use of *kappō*, which can be used to revive an unconscious, dead, or near-death opponent. One modern interpretation of *kappō* would be the use of CPR (Cardio Pulmonary Resuscitation); *kappō* techniques were not widely known, so shrouded in mysticism and secrecy. *"Kappō was used in the battlefields and during duels between clans and schools. Applying it to not only samurai of the same side, but also to keep the enemy alive, among other purposes to force interrogation or torture."*[107]

Figure 13 – Example of kappō in use

[106] Gluck, (1973), *Zen Combat*, p.80
[107] Caracena, (2017), *Tenjin Shinyo Ryu JuJitsu*, p.119

Yin and Yang

The concept of *yin* and *yang* is important to Japanese martial philosophy. *Yin* and *yang* comes from ancient Chinese philosophy: that the universe is made up of sets of complementary opposites, hard and soft, night and day, black and white, male and female; *yin* and *yang*. *Yin* and *yang* thus represents the continual process of change. For example, day (*yang*) is forever turning to night (*yin*) and night is forever turning to day. The tai chi diagram of *yin* and *yang* below is the best illustrative interpretation of this philosophy. Note how they are entering each other's half of the circle and *yin* is actually inside *yang* and vice versa.

Figure 14 – Tai chi representation of yin and yang

Discovering in practice that being calm and centered, whilst *uke* attacks furiously in an uncontrolled manner allows the effectiveness of *tori's* jūjutsu technique to be at its most poignant. This is just one way of discovering the *yin* and *yang* relationship between a calm mind and a fast, effective technique.

Some jūjutsu instructors will refer to *yin* and *yang* as a concept. For example, when *uke* pushes, *tori* must pull. This can be taught using the concept of *yin* and *yang*, rather than 'push and pull' so the next time the same concept comes up in training - for example, meeting force with softness, the instructor can use the same phrase, '*yin* and *yang*', and the connection for the student is more easily absorbed.

Chapter 4: Physicality

身体性

Jūjutsu Technique

Learning a jūjutsu technique is more than just going through the physical motions and memorising the technique in one dimension. An experienced *jūjutsuka* will apply balance, timing, posture, speed, coordination and experience to allow the principles of each technique to work in a variety of different situations. Learning jūjutsu proficiently requires both physical and mental discipline alongside continuing purposeful practice.

Jūjutsu can be studied from three standpoints: *waza* (technique), *shin* (mind and spirit) and *ki* (an intangible strength that comes from within).

Jūjutsu techniques can be broken down broadly as shown in Table 15.

Table 15 – Broad techniques of jūjutsu

Balance	Stances	Breakfalls	Blocking
Atemi waza	Hand strikes	Kicking	Elbow and knee strikes
Locking	Ground work	Throwing	Circular motion and common principles
Chokes and strangles	Evasive movement	Counters	Combinations
Escaping from holds	Pressure points	Kata	First aid and kuatsu

Modern research and understanding has discovered that it takes 10,000 hours of purposeful practice to become an 'expert' in any given field[108]. Natural talent is no substitute. What the *jūjutsuka* needs to be aware of is that practice is indeed 'purposeful' and pushing the students boundaries each and every time.

Balance
The majority of jūjutsu techniques rely on the opponent being off balance to work efficiently. This off balancing is called kuzushi. The jūjutsu principle of **minimum effort for maximum effect**₃ relies heavily on kuzushi. Kuzushi can be achieved in several ways, but generally follows; striking, pushing, pulling and applying pressure to vulnerable areas (including pressure points and joint locks).

---

[108] Syed, (2011), Bounce, p.12

Stances

Jūjutsuka are trained to stand in a certain way, serving several purposes both defensively and offensively. Types of stances are shown below.

Table 16 – Jūjutsu stances

Zenkutsu dachi	Forward stance
Kiba dachi	Horse riding stance
Fudo dachi	Rooted stance
Hachiji dachi	Natural stance
Kokutsu dachi	Back stance
Neko ashi dachi	Cat stance

The Japanese word for posture is *kamae*. A confident fighting stance can project a strength which, even on its own, could be enough to avoid conflict. Stances can portray years of training and radiate the mental strength a student has developed in preparation to defend themselves. On the other hand, the *jūjutsuka* may purposely adopt a weaker stance to hide their training and gain the element of surprise prior to conflict. Stances can be left or right-handed depending on the student's natural preference.

Break Falls

The first thing a *jūjutsuka* must learn are the *ukemi waza* (break falls). In jūjutsu this means that for 50% of the time, the student is playing the part of *uke*. Learning to fall and land properly should be a continual focus of training. As students progress through the belts and the throws become more advanced, so the break falling must keep pace. This is to be practiced constantly to avoid injury. Break falls should be practiced with increasing intensity in correlation with the student's grade to discover and rectify any flaws in technique.

The jūjutsu break fall disperses the energy of a throw over as large an area of the *tatami* as possible whilst positioning the body in such a way that the most delicate joints and anatomical areas are protected from the impact of the fall. *"Instead of avoiding the ground, try to hit is with as many square inches of surface as possible"*[109] *Uke* should exhale sharply at the moment of impact to prevent being winded.

The most common break falls in jūjutsu are shown in Table 17.

---

[109] Miyake & Tani (1906), The Game of Ju-jitsu, p.19

Table 17 – Common jūjutsu breakfalls

Yoko ukemi	Sideways fall
Ushiro ukemi	Backwards fall
Mae ukemi	Front fall
Zenpō Kaiten	Forward roll
Ushiro Kaiten	Backwards roll

Blocking

Uke-waza (blocking techniques) are a regularly used set of jūjutsu techniques which are trained at every session. The main blocking techniques are shown in Table 18.

Table 18 – Main blocking techniques

Age uke	Rising block
Epi uke	Elbow block
Gedan barai	Downward sweeping block
Jōdan jūji uke	Rising cross block
Gedan jūji uke	Downward cross block
Shuto uke	Knife hand block
Soto uke	Outside forearm block
Suki uke	Scooping block
Ude uke	Inside forearm block

Blocking in jūjutsu is often referred to as 'trapping' due to its dual purpose leading *tori* into other techniques. Where possible, jūjutsu favors the use of blocking techniques that yield to the opponent's strength by, for example, diverting the strike whilst avoiding the blow and countering with *tori's* own strike using the *uke's* weight and direction of force to *tori's* advantage.

Meeting force with force will only result in the bigger, stronger opponent winning the outcome. A strike will nearly always follow a block in jūjutsu, as a finishing move or as a way into *kuzushi* for the next technique.

In a real self-defence situation, it is very likely that each party will receive several blows regardless of their blocking prowess. The *jūjutsuka* should train to appreciate and negate the effects of these strikes, or surprise attacks, whilst keeping a focus on driving their own agenda to land the final technique to win the bout. Each block should be used as a way into an attack.

Morally and legally it is best to let the opponent initiate the attack. Pre-emptive striking (avoiding the block altogether), however, can create an opening to overcome the opponent more easily and with less risk to the *tori*. As espoused by Redenbach (2008) *"Action beats re-action every time"*[110] meaning those who strike first land the first strike and take the advantage from there, the opponent may never get another chance, especially with a weapon.

Atemi-Waza

Atemi-waza (striking techniques) are subdivided in this section into; punching and hand strikes, kicking, and elbow and knee strikes.

Punching and Hand Strikes

The Japanese word for punch is *tsuki*. On first reflection, a strike may seem obvious but in fact years of training are required to perfect these techniques.

The hand has 27 individual bones and perfecting strikes with proper technique will help to strengthen and protect these bones. Jūjutsu emphasises using a hard target such as bone, striking a softer target such as flesh. Bone to bone strikes do not play to the strengths of jūjutsu.

The shape and technique of the strike should be specific to the target area being attacked. Experience will result in the correct technique being subconsciously selected in the sub-seconds before impact. Jabbing with the fingers to vulnerable areas such as the eyes and throat can be devastating even with a small amount of applied force. Common strikes studied in jūjutsu are shown in Table 19.

Table 19 – Types of jūjutsu striking techniques

Gyaku-zuki	Reverse punch
Oi-suki	Jab
Age-zuki	Upper cut
Mawashi-zuki	Hook
Haitō uchi	Ridge hand
Kaishō	Open hand
Tettsui-uchi	Hammer fist
Nihon-nukite	Finger strike
Nukite	Spear hand
Oyayubi ippon ken	Thumb first knuckle
Teisho-uchi	Palm heel

---

[110] Redenbach, (2008), Waveman

| Uraken-uchi | Back fist |

Atemi (striking vulnerable areas) is taught in many jūjutsu schools. Some schools focus on anatomical striking, others on *atemi* strikes and others teach a combination of both. *Atemi* points can include pressure points, joints, eyes, throat, arteries and nerve endings. There is further information on this in the anatomy section. In jūjutsu every part of the body can be used as a weapon.

Kicking

A kick can be very powerful and can easily incapacitate the opponent. The Japanese terminology for kicking techniques is *keri waza*. Other arts such as taekwondo and savate rely much more heavily on kicking; in jūjutsu the main kicking techniques are shown in Table 20.

Table 20 - Types of jūjutsu kicking techniques

Mae geri	Front kick
Mawashi geri	Roundhouse kick
Ushiro geri	Back kick
Yoko geri keage	Side kick

The use of overly fanciful kicks is not generally part of the jūjutsu syllabus. Kicks in jūjutsu tend to stay below the waist and focus on temporarily incapacitating the opponent or attacking vulnerable joints such as the knees. As jūjutsu is not a sporting art, it is far more effective to hyper-extend the opponent's knee than to leave yourself vulnerable by going for a kick to the head. In this case, less is more. Jūjutsu also teaches defending from kicks when both standing and on the ground.

Elbow and Knee Strikes

Jūjutsu is effective from kicking range to grappling range, to ground distance and the *jūjutsuka* favours close combat at a range where elbows and knees can be very effective for striking. Elbow and knee strikes are equally effective from both standing and groundwork. At fighting distances common in jūjutsu the knee strike is not only extremely powerful but can also be more balanced and carry more weight than a kick. Elbows and knees can be very effective at producing a powerful block and are an essential part of the jūjutsu syllabus.

Locking

In jūjutsu locking or *kansetsu-waza* forms a major part of the syllabus of techniques. Along with throwing, it was one of the few unarmed techniques a *samurai* could perform on a fully armoured opponent. Joint locks include fingers, wrists, arms, elbows, shoulders, feet, ankles, legs and neck.

Performing a lock involves isolating the opponent's joint and applying pressure through leverage to move the joint up to its full range of motion, and beyond if desired or appropriate. In a restraint situation, it is possible to hyperextend a joint, causing pain to the opponent in such a controlled way that compliance is achieved through pain without causing any permanent damage to the joint. In a combat situation, joint locks target muscle, tendon and ligament damage, dislocation or fractures.

Locks can be applied to the larger joints such as the knees and hips and to smaller joints such as fingers and thumbs. Wristlocks are an especially useful technique in jūjutsu as they can subdue, control or maim an opponent. As soon as *uke* feels the pressure of the lock they should tap either themselves, the *tatami* or *tori* to indicate that *tori* must release the lock immediately. It is good to build up tolerance by resisting locks, but even better to stay injury-free and be able to train.

Ground Work
Jūjutsu includes various techniques for *Ne-waza* (ground work) against single and multiple attackers. This concept has been taken much further by Brazilian jiu jitsu, although with BJJ and jūdō multiple attackers are not generally trained for whereas they are in jūjutsu.

Throwing
Nage-waza (throwing techniques), like locking techniques could be used on a *samurai* warrior in full armour. *Nage-waza* are broken down into sub-sections of hip, neck, leg, front, back, side, rear, dropping and sacrifice.

A jūjutsu throw generally involves breaking the opponent's balance (*kuzushi*) or weakening them through strikes before executing the throw.

Throwing techniques must go in order; *kuzushi* (off balancing), *tsukuri* (entry to technique) and *kake* (execution of the technique). Inexperienced *jūjutsuka* may try straight for *kake* which will often result in failure. This step-by-step process will become increasingly fluid and unconsciously available to *tori* with increasing experience and continuous training.

There are over 50 throws that would be a starting point for a full *goshin* jūjutsu syllabus; a set of techniques that would take years to learn.

Circular Motion and Common Principles

In jūjutsu *tori* becomes the centre of a sphere of energy created by *uke*. Centrifugal and centripetal forces are overcome by using the *uke's* force and redirecting it to *tori's* own advantage.

Chokes and Strangles

Shime-waza (constriction techniques) can be divided between 'chokes' and 'strangles,' which are anatomically different, and the trained *jūjutsuka* will use them for different reasons in differing situations. Both methods involve applying pressure to the neck to starve the brain of oxygen. Results can vary from coughing to unconsciousness or death. It is entirely possible to apply a choke and a strangle at the same time.

Strangulation techniques involve restricting blood flow to the brain by compressing the carotid arteries or the jugular veins. The airway is left clear in a pure strangle.

The brain needs oxygen to function, by reducing the oxygen in the blood the brain goes into a hypoxic (lack of oxygen) state. The body tries to protect itself by going into unconsciousness to reduce its oxygen need and hence *uke* is 'knocked out'. The whole technique can take between three and eight seconds to perform and should be released (in a self-defence scenario) immediately once the opponent loses consciousness. Keeping the strangle applied after this point can cause permanent damage or death. A strangle comes on gradually over the seconds it is applied, and the opponent will gradually lose a grip on vision and consciousness. Strangles are often referred to as 'blood chokes', this is one and the same thing.

Choking techniques have the same end result as strangles, that is hypoxia of the brain. But instead of restricting oxygen via the blood veins and arteries, oxygen is restricted at the point of intake via the larynx, or trachea. Unlike a strangle, the choke comes on instantaneously, often resulting in a flurry of panic from the opponent.

Evasive Movement

Jūjutsu favours avoidance and redirection of the opponent's strength over meeting force-with-force. This allows the smaller, weaker opponent to triumph over the larger, stronger one.

The physical movement and reading of the attack to evade is called *tai sabaki*. *Tai sabaki* is just a small (and often subconscious) skill set of the trained *jūjutsuka*. Anticipation is a side benefit from years of training. Experience with violence or fighting provides the proponent with a wider awareness of an oncoming threat. *Tai sabaki* (evasive movement) is an ideal training tool as each jūjutsu technique should be taught and practiced from multiple angles of attack and subsequent variations on defensive technique.

Counters
Generally speaking, it is preferable to counter before the attack which, although less defendable in court of law would be more advantageous in actual conflict.

Why risk being hit when you can hit first when action beats re-action every time? Of course, counter techniques in jūjutsu are not just about strikes, but most *ryū* will teach counters to every type of technique giving the student the growing ability to move seamlessly from one technique to the next.

Jūjutsu is primarily designed to benefit from responding to an attacker's force with technique, so in this way jūjutsu works most effectively in a defensive situation, not as the aggressor.

Combinations
Much like counters, combinations are a symbol of the advanced jūjutsu student. The ability to seamlessly flow from one technique to the next keeps the opponent on the back foot, and should eventually lead to execution of a technique (or several techniques) that will enable the *jūjutsuka* to overcome their opponent successfully.

Escaping from Holds
Part of a typical *goshin* jūjutsu syllabus involves escaping when held by the opponent. This could be via the wrist, around the waist, by the neck, hair, ankles or any other form of effective grip to body or clothing. These escapes are taught statically in varying scenarios; an advanced student can unpeel all the escape techniques they have been taught to enable them to flow from technique to technique seamlessly.

Pressure Points
The body contains many vulnerable areas. Although pressure point locations are similar in every person, the effectiveness of striking the same point in different people will differ greatly.

Jūjutsuka should always apply pressure point strikes with an anatomical backup in mind. If the primary target (the pressure point) is ineffective, then the joint or soft surrounding area will still incur some damage. Pressure points are only used by senior grades as they require a good level of self-control and accuracy to be safe and effective.

Kata

Kata is used in jūjutsu to practice sequences of movements and techniques. It can be done solo or with one or more attackers. *Kata* provides a way for students to develop physical memory, sequencing and motor learning. *Kata* should always be taught with and without contact to learn the context of the movement.

The danger with *kata* is it becomes a dance with no practical application. Working with application (i.e., with an *uke*) or genuinely visualising (making it real in the student's own mind), the opponent helps keep *kata* as a useful martial training method. *Kata* is commonly practiced in jūjutsu with and without weapons.

Draeger (1973) reiterates the importance of *kata* in maintaining proficiency when deadly techniques cannot be practiced in real combat. *"[Kata] … is the only way by which the action that characterizes the bujutsu can be practiced without the practitioner's being wounded or killed."*[111]

First Aid and Kuatsu

Whilst *jūjutsuka* are learning to harm, they can also be adept at learning to heal. With the amassed knowledge of anatomy and experience of dealing with injuries, senior students tend to be particularly good at first aid. Resuscitation is usually commonplace on the jūjutsu syllabus.

Kuatsu (or *kwappo*) originally relates to 28 methods of resuscitation, body massage, bone setting and joint manipulation based on the Taoist philosophy of *yin* and *yang*. Brought from China to Japan in around 1530, they were incorporated into the Yoshin ryū (willow hearted school) by Yoshi Shirobei Akiyama.

Burgin describes the use of *Kuatsu* in an 1892 article for the London Idler: *"Kuatsu, which means to resuscitate, is the art of resuscitating those who have apparently died through violence … The art of resuscitation was considered a secret, and all pupils had to take a solemn oath not to reveal it."*[112]

---

[111] Draeger, (1973), *Classical Bujutsu*, p.56
[112] Burgin, (1892), *The Idler*, p.281-286

As various styles of jūjutsu exist and continue to be created, jūjutsu can be thought of like a tree, the roots representing **early classical jūjutsu**, the basics of the art common to all styles. The trunk represents the Edo (**late classical**) style; the branches, some older than others, some large, some small, represent the different *ryū*. The leaves of the jūjutsu tree represent the individual's personal style and interpretation.

<u>Anatomy</u>

"Physical strength is of secondary importance to knowledge of the human body, its muscles, nerves and arteries. 'Knowledge is power.'"[113]

Unarmed combat can be approached from two main strategies, landing a hard blow to the opponent's body or applying pressure across a joint. Jūjutsu uses both of these principles in the most efficient way possible. For example, a disproportionate amount of pain or damage can be caused by landing blows to specific areas. A strike to the genitals, or throat for example will deliver greater effect for the same force than a strike to a large muscle group.

"The special feature of this art [jujutsu] *is that its efficiency depends not on strength, but on skill and quickness of movement, combined with the knowledge of certain facts about the human body"*[114]

Leverage across the most vulnerable joints incapacitates an opponent for a relatively small amount of force, the same force across a different joint may have zero effect. Anatomical knowledge, therefore, is the difference between the use of strength, technique and speed being effective or not. In a situation where the victim only gets one chance, the difference could be capture, loss, or death.

"In order to become skilled in jiu-jitsu, a thorough knowledge of the location of the muscles, bones and arteries of the human body is necessary"[115]

Anatomical knowledge is essential for a student to progress in jūjutsu, especially through the *dan* grades. The following is a basic starting point for jūjutsu students, to help provide a springboard for further in-depth study. Knowledge of anatomy is useful when intending to harm, heal or condition the body. A basic understanding of anatomy will also give the student the confidence to commit to jūjutsu techniques with a heightened awareness of the likely outcome of the application of that particular technique.

From a traditional Western perspective, medicine emphasises modern scientific methods while traditionally the Eastern concept of medicine is based on a 3,000-

---

[113] Skinner, (1904), *Jiu-Jitsu – The Japanese Method of Attack and Self Defense*, p.4

[114] Sutherland, (1916), *Ju-Jitsu: Self Defence*, p.22

[115] (1959), Jiu-Jitsu, The Japanese Art of Wrestling and Self Defence, p.9

year-old philosophical approach that focuses on a more holistic and energetic concept of the human body. Knowledge of both approaches would be invaluable to the progressing *jūjutsuka*.

In the Eastern approach to the human body, much reference to the concept of *ki* is found, which is described in further detail later.

The Spinal Column
The spinal column is composed of a series of bones called 'vertebrae' stacked on one another.

If the nerve that runs down the spinal column is damaged or severed (this can be caused as a secondary consequence of breaking or dislodging the vertebrae), paralysis of the body can occur. The higher up the break, the greater the loss of movement will be. *Tori* should take great care with *uke* never to damage the spine. Good break falls will also help to protect the spine when falling.

Figure 15 – Vertebral column

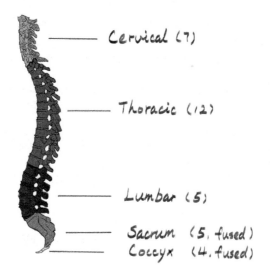

The Skeleton

The skeleton is what keeps the human body upright and provides a chassis for all the other components of the body to attach to and drive movement. The skeleton can be divided down into the axial (rib cage, spine and head) and the appendicular (the limbs).

Figure 16 – 206 named bones of the human skeleton

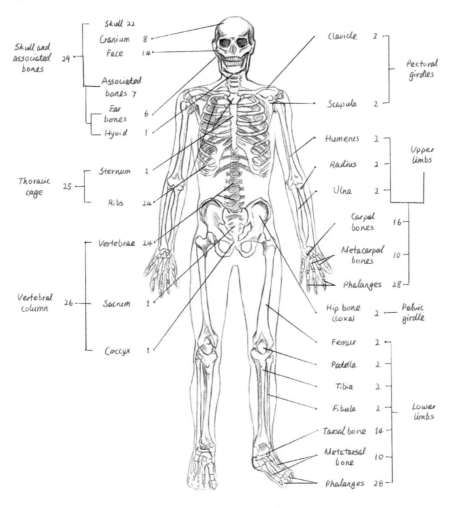

The body has 206 named bones which jūjutsu students should become increasingly familiar with as they progress their journey through the belts.

Table 21 – 206 named bones of the human body

Spine (vertebral column)	Cervical vertebrae	7
	Thoracic vertebrae	12
	Lumbar vertebrae	5
	Sacrum	1
	Coccyx	1
Chest (thorax)	Sternum	1
	Ribs	24
Skull / Head	Cranial bones	8
	Facial bones	14
	Hyoid bone	1
	Middle ears	6
Upper Limbs	Humerus	2
	Scapula	2
	Clavicle	2
	Ulna	2
	Radius	2
	Hand	54
Pelvis	Pelvic girdle	2
Lower Limbs	Femur	2
	Patella or kneecap	2
	Tibia	2
	Fibula	2
	Foot	52

Joints

Knowledge of the body's joints and their range and direction of motion is fundamental to the jūjutsu student as the majority of locking techniques rely on this knowledge to be applied effectively and/or safely. Joints can be defined in terms of their movement characteristics.

'Fibrous' or 'sutural' joints have no movement at all (that is of any use to *a jūjutsuka*). These joints are found in the skull and pelvis.

'Cartilaginous' joints only move very slightly in isolation but tend to be grouped together so the effect of them all moving at once can actually generate a greater range of movement. Examples can be found in the spine and in the hands and feet.

'Synovial' joints have the greatest range of movement and all generally rely on a capsule of fluid (called synovium) to lubricate and nourish the joint. The joint is also lined with cartilage to reduce friction and protect the joint ends. In jūjutsu the student learns to feel these joints out instinctively during combat and reverse them to create pain or immobilisation. Typical examples would be the elbows, knees and shoulders.

Ligaments

A ligament is a fibrous tissue used to hold muscles to bones. Ligaments are commonly injured in sport and can heal naturally if stretched or torn. A completely severed or ripped ligament will need surgical intervention to heal.

Muscles

There are approximately 215 pairs of muscles arranged symmetrically down each side of the body. Muscles can only pull, and not push so always work in pairs - otherwise there would be no way to reverse the action. Opposing muscles also help keep movements smooth by tensioning and controlling both sides of the action.

When activated, the cells in a muscle contract and slide past one another, producing a contraction that changes the length and shape of the muscle. Muscles can be voluntary (e.g. leg muscle) or involuntary (e.g. heart muscle). The muscles in Table 22 work in pairs. The muscles making the main movement by contracting are referred to as the 'agonists' and the opposing muscle known as the 'protagonists' will relax to allow their counterparts to move. During this process, other muscles known as 'synergists' will assist with the desired movement.

Figure 17 – Major muscle groups

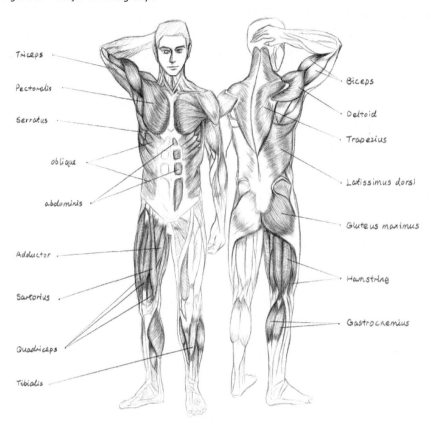

Triceps

Pectoralis

Serratus

oblique

abdominis

Adductor

Sartorius

Quadriceps

Tibialis

Biceps

Deltoid

Trapezius

Latissimus dorsi

Gluteus maximus

Hamstring

Gastrocnemius

The basic function of the muscles illustrated in Figure 17 are shown in Table 22.

Table 22 - Basic functions of the main muscle groups

Triceps	Extend the forearm at the elbow
Pectorals	Draw the arm forward and in toward the body
Serratus	Draws the shoulder blade forward, helps raise the arm and assist in pushing
Oblique	Assists in the lateral rotation of the trunk
Abdominals	Depress the chest cavity, compress the abdomen, bend the backbone
Adductors	Flex, laterally rotates and draw the thigh towards the body
Sartorius	Bends the thigh at the hip, bends the lower leg at the knee, rotates the thigh in an outward direction
Quadriceps	Flexes the thigh at the hips, extends the leg at the knee
Tibialis	Flexes the foot towards the shin
Biceps	Flexes the forearm at the elbow
Deltoid	Raises the arm
Trapezius	Lifts the shoulder blade, braces the shoulder, draws the head back
Latissimus Dorsi	Rotates and draws the arm backwards and towards the body
Gluteus	Extends and rotates the thigh outward
Hamstring	Draws the thigh backward, flexes the knee
Gastrocnemius	Bends the lower leg at the knee, extends the foot when jumping

The Respiratory System

It is important to have a basic understanding of the respiratory system as some of the techniques in jūjutsu are designed to damage or impair this vital lifeline. The organs detailed below are responsible for taking in oxygen from the air around us to deliver to the body via the lungs, and expel carbon dioxide created in the body back into the atmosphere.

Figure 18 – Respiratory system

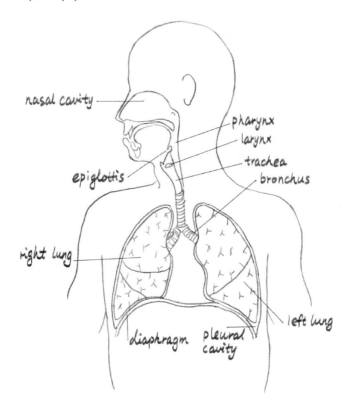

The Circulatory System

With the heart at the centre of the circulatory system, a *jūjutsuka* would benefit from a basic understanding of where arteries appear near the skin's surface and can become vulnerable to striking and sharp weapons.

Figure 19 – Circulatory system

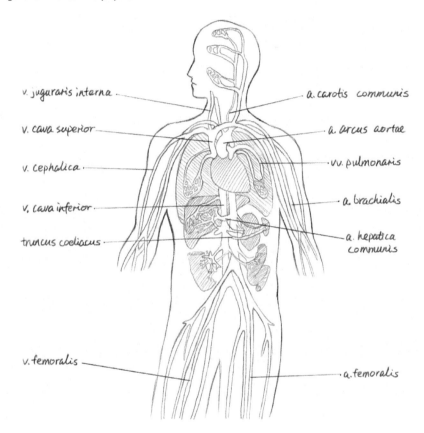

Pressure Points

There are areas on the body that when pressure is applied with the correct location, angle and force, can induce differing results. Focused pressure can be applied to tendons, ligaments and muscles to induce pain and distract or immobilise the opponent. Applying pressure to a 'reflex point' can cause involuntary movement which can be used to temporarily release grip, destroy balance or in some cases cause unconsciousness.

Striking areas are differentiated from pressure points and have different uses in different scenarios. Compliance techniques can involve the use of pressure points to encourage compliance from a passively resisting opponent. If the situation escalates, striking to vital areas can be incorporated with the appropriate level of force.

Pressure points are a specialised area of jūjutsu. Further information can be sought from dedicated resources.

Atemi Points

Another common name for atemi points in Chinese is *dim mak*, also known in Japanese as *kyūsho*. *Atemi* points are vital striking areas where the body has weak areas that can be effectively attacked with a disproportionate force-to-result ratio.

Scientific understanding of the body's vital areas enables the *jūjutsuka* to make the most effective and efficient use of each technique. Each encounter will be different, so striking areas can be selected taking into account the opponent's clothing, local conditions, number of attackers and the nature of the encounter.

Striking areas are often referred to as *atemi* points and practiced in jūjutsu under the broader *atemi-waza* techniques.

Figure 20 – Atemi points

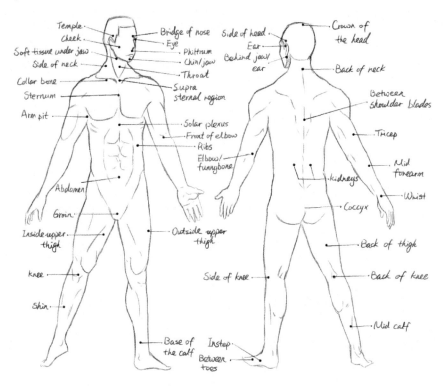

Ki

Ki is a medically intangible life force familiar to some practitioners of the martial arts. The art of *kiai-jutsu* is dedicated to this art. *Ki* originates in the human body from the *saika tanden*, which is found about 30mm below the navel. Familiar to the martial arts of India, China and Japan, *Ki* (or *Qi*) roughly translates as 'breath.' *Ki* is channeled through the body by concentration, focus and relaxation.

Absorbing blows from the opponent is called *in ki* whilst *yo ki* is the ability to strike with the aid of *ki*.

Human Physical Evolution

Jūjutsu is as effective on today's city streets as it was on the ancient battlefields of Japan. Whilst the rest of the world has changed around us, why has jūjutsu kept its effectiveness? The answer is because human biomechanics have not changed and we can only work with (and against) the bodies we are given. *"Because the ancestors of all modern humans were still living in the heat of Africa as little as*

100,000 years ago and most evolutionary adaptations move very slowly." [116]
Essentially the process of using the human body as a weapon in unarmed combat
has remained consistent for over 100,000 years.

Modern humans are 99.90% per cent identical to our ancestors of 40,000 years
ago. Our ancestors of 15,000 years ago are 99.95% per cent similar to our present-
day selves.[117]

It is not therefore unrealistic to imagine that every 'new' modern technique in
jūjutsu is actually just a rediscovery of a technique that has been used either
intentionally or unintentionally at some point in human history. There are only so
many ways the body can move or be restrained, destroyed or damaged. All jūjutsu
is really doing is enabling the organised teaching and practice of these techniques.

---

[116] Stroud, (2004), *Survival of the Fittest*, p.203
[117] Stroud, (2004), *Survival of the Fittest*.

Fitness

The core principle of jūjutsu is that the smaller, weaker person can triumph over the larger, stronger one by using technique and knowledge to overcome brute strength. In his 1907 book, Uyenishi states *"the inner truth of Ju-jutsu, the victor establishing the superiority of leverage and balance, two soft, delicate qualities, over the harder, rougher ones of strength and force."*[118]

"It must always be borne in mind that the whole fabric of Ju-jitsu is based on the utilisation of strategy, agility and rapidity of movement, rather than on strength pure and simple. Success is achieved rather by the conservation of energy than by the use of it. There is a proverb to the effect that 'knowledge is power,' and knowledge of Ju-jitsu is the beginning and end of power."[119]

Of course, this is not a guaranteed formula and foregoing luck; a greater mixture of technique, knowledge, fitness and strength would tip the odds largely in favour of the fitter more prepared fighter. Having practice and knowledge of good technique should be the core of a *jūjutsuka's* training which is balanced equally with training for speed, flexibility, strength and stamina.

The desired blend of fitness and technique is as old as jūjutsu itself; *"...the royal road to good health, and perfection in training. 'Mens Sana in corpore sano' (a sound mind in a sound body) [Latin]."*[120]

With a limitation on time, it is important to know early on which areas of exercise fitness will complement jūjutsu most efficiently and effectively.

Speed
Having mastered the techniques of jūjutsu, students must keep practicing and drilling technique to work on speed.

Slow is smooth, smooth is fast.

Speed is a natural development that comes with time and practice, confidence and ability. Fitness is not essential to jūjutsu, but a fitter fighter with the same

---

[118] Uyenishi, (1940), *The Textbook of Ju-Jutsu as Practised in Japan*, p.14
[119] Uyenishi, (1940), *The Textbook of Ju-Jutsu as Practised in Japan*, p.22
[120] Bankier, (1905), *Ju-Jitsu, What it Really Is*, p.18

knowledge is always going to have an advantage over the fighter who neglects fitness.

"Jiu-Jitsu does not demand muscular development to the same extent that it is needed in the practice of boxing or wrestling, but it is well –and very nearly absolutely essential- to possess nerves and muscles that are especially trained to respond with lightning-like swiftness to the demands that are put upon them by the peculiarities of the Japanese style of personal encounter."[121]

Flexibility

Some of the more advanced jūjutsu techniques require a high level of flexibility, which will become more prevalent with age. *Jūjutsuka* should be constantly working to maintain and improve their flexibility. This can be done on and off the *tatami* and at virtually any place and any time. Turning and twisting exercises will help increase range of movement and can be done with a partner. Flexibility will also help the *jūjutsuka* to mitigate injury.

Strength

It is not necessary for the jūjutsu student to work with big weights, expensive equipment or hours of gym time. In fact, this could have a detrimental effect on speed, flexibility and stamina. Good technique will allow the *jūjutsuka* to lift and throw virtually all opponents, so strength should be derived from bodyweight exercises such as press-ups, pull-ups, sit-ups, squats and such-like.

"When opposed to one physically stronger than yourself do not be afraid and, on the other hand, never despise one weaker than yourself. Do not recklessly resist your opponent's physical strength; imitate the action of a boat adrift upon the surface of the ocean."[122]

Jūjutsu is the 'gentle art' and relies on off-balancing the opponent, using *uke's* push to reinforce *tori's* pull. Executing technique with perfect timing and placement during that moment just before the opponent realises they are about to fall straight into a trap. Musashi Minyamoto, one of the great *samurai* swordsmen of all time says of timing; *"You win battles with the timing in the void born of the*

---

[121] Hancock, (1904), *Jiu-Jitsu Combat Tricks*, p.2
[122] Hancock, (1950), *The Fighting Spirit of Japan*, p.38

timing of cunning by knowing the enemies' timing, and thus using a timing which the enemy does not expect." [123]

Stamina

Stamina can be practiced directly through jūjutsu practice in the *dōjō* or can be supplemented outside of the *dōjō*. Repetition of stepping into and out of techniques (known as *uchi komi*) is a great way of building stamina, speed and technique at the same time. Working on *nage-waza* (ground techniques) also follows a similar path and is a great way of resistance training and stamina building. Punch bag and focus mitts can also build stamina alongside speed and technique.

Low-intensity aerobic exercise will increase overall fitness and take the *jūjutsuka* to the next level with stamina. Regular distance running, swimming or cycling are also great ways to build stamina.

Conditioning

Jūjutsuka are able to toughen their hands and feet by striking repetition and the body is conditioned for the impact of being thrown by repeated practice of break falls. Conditioning can be achieved over a lifetime through practice, patience and endeavor. Trying to condition too quickly can risk structural damage to the body.

Warming up for Practice

Warming up before jūjutsu practice is an essential way to mitigate injury. It is important to know how and why this is the case. By raising the body's temperature and heart rate, the temperature in the muscles rises, circulating the fluid between the joints. This decreases the chances of the bones grinding against each other, and reduces the risk of pulls and strains in muscles. Keeping the muscles warm and prepared for exercise helps to prevent any sudden acute injuries from a sudden overuse.

The enzymes in muscles work best at 38 degrees Celsius. Before warming up they will be about 37 degrees and it takes a good level of exercise (two miles of gentle jogging for comparison) to reach 38 degrees. Time should be reserved at the end of a training session for a warm down which will help relax tightened muscles and prepare for leaving the *dōjō* with a clear head.

---

[123] Musashi, (2012), *A Book of Five Rings*, p.41

The Laws of Physics Applied to Jūjutsu

With appropriate jūjutsu training and technique, the smaller, weaker person can defeat the bigger, stronger opponent. The syllabus of a proficient *jūjutsuka* will include these simple lessons of physics which can be taught and applied to jūjutsu techniques.

Sir Isaac Newton (1643-1727) studied and set down the laws of physics concerning motion. Newton defined motion as 'mass that is changing position', and his three laws of motion are important principles in jūjutsu.

Newton's First Law: Inertia

"An object at rest, or not in motion, will stay that way unless acted on by an unbalanced force"

In jūjutsu, the smaller, lighter fighter needs to produce enough force to overcome the inertia of the heavy fighter. This is achieved by using the heavy fighter's weight against them. The *jūjutsuka* can use a smaller force to move the bigger opponent by taking them off balance which, in effect, is the *uke* helping move themselves by putting their body weight in the same direction *tori* is now pushing or pulling.

Newton's Second Law: F=MA

"Force = Mass x Acceleration"

For a force to exist, it must have a mass (its weight) and an acceleration (its speed). Imagine a hand strike in jūjutsu, the mass being a fist. The weight of the fist cannot change so the only way to generate a larger force is by speed and technique. The proficient *jūjutsuka* learns how to generate more force by putting more body weight behind the strike and through training and good technique the acceleration can be greatly improved.

Newton's Third Law: Action-Reaction

"For every action there is an equal and opposite reaction"

Striking an immovable object for example a wall would mean all the force put into that strike would be directed back into the hand and arm, and will quite probably break bones, diminishing proficiency, should *tori* need to fight again straight after.

The reaction of the strike would change if something much lighter was hit, such as a boxing speedball. With the ball being so light the force (mass multiplied by acceleration) of the strike would only have been in contact with the ball for a very small amount of time before overcoming its inertia. Once this is achieved, more of the force from the strike can be used for moving the ball than for coming back into the hand. This is important in jūjutsu as, to apply the most effective possible technique, *tori* must be conscious of the reaction (to both *tori* and *uke*) that the strike or technique is going to produce.

Archimedes: Principles of Leverage

Archimedes; an ancient Greek mathematician (c287 BC-c212 BC) was the first to document the principle of a lever:

> *"A lever amplifies an input force to provide a greater output force. The ratio of the output force to the input force is the mechanical advantage of the lever."*

Levers are fundamental to the jūjutsu principle of the smaller, weaker opponent being able to defeat the larger, heavier aggressor. By combining the principles of leverage and a knowledge of anatomy, the *jūjutsuka* can subdue, break bones and even kill their opponent with relatively minimal effort.

First-Class Lever

A first-class lever can be demonstrated by *tori* facing *uke* and putting a hand behind to press firmly on the back of his *obi* thus creating the fulcrum. The load is the weight of *uke* on the floor through the soles of his/her feet. Tilting the head back with *tori's* other hand under *uke's* chin will represent the applied effort. Getting *uke* off balance or even causing them to fall requires very little effort using this first class lever method.

Figure 21 – First-class lever

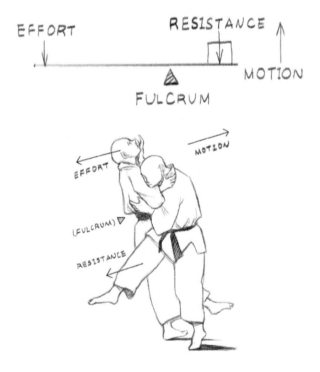

Second-Class Lever

Using the example of a finger lock in jūjutsu, a second-class lever would be the most efficient way to easily and effectively break the finger back. Pushing down above the middle joint in the finger, whilst simultaneously using *tori's* thumb to create a fulcrum as close to the base of *uke's* finger as possible and lifting with *tori's* index finger, *tori* creates a lever and easily causes pain.

Figure 22 – Second-class lever

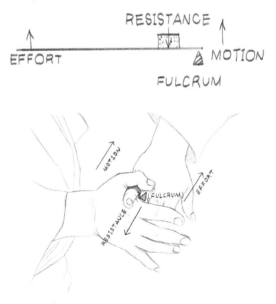

Third-Class Lever

An overhead weapon strike would use the third class lever principle, rotating the weapon with the grip creating both the fulcrum and the lever, and the opposite end of the weapon becomes the load. The lever is very effective in this situation and can generate a lot of acceleration at the end of the weapon. As can be seen from Newton's second law, this can turn the relatively small weight of the weapon into a great force. The advanced *jūjutsuka* combines these two principles with experienced technique and anatomical knowledge, to devastating effect.

Figure 23 – Third-class lever

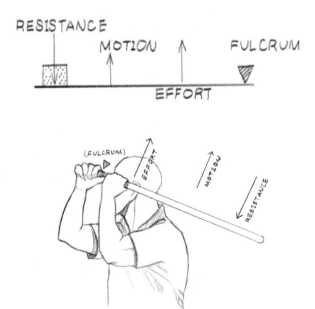

Chapter 5: Progeny

Jūjutsu Family Tree

Figure 24 – Jūjutsu family tree

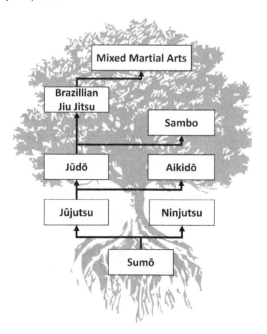

The *Nihon shoki* (chronicle of Japan), a document from 720 AD mentions *sumō* as a form of competitive grappling, this pre-dates any mention of jūjutsu. Whilst the *samurai* used jūjutsu to complement their primary weapons techniques *sumō* developed as a pure grappling form becoming popular in the Japanese imperial court and with the *daimyō*.

Jigorō Kanō codified jūdō in1882 and Morihei Ueshiba codified aikido in 1920s, both were both jūjutsu masters before forming their own arts based on the techniques of jūjutsu.

Karate did not come from jūjutsu but is a widely popular Japanese martial art developed by Gichin Funakoshi in 1922, (founder of Shotokan karate) based on earlier karate forms from Okinawa. It is interesting to note that jūjutsu has been in Britain longer than Karate has been in Japan.

Russian sambo wrestling was developed by Vasili Oshchepov and Viktor Spiridonov in 1938 for the Soviet military, both men having trained and taken influence from jūdō amongst other arts.

Brazilian jiu jitsu, developed by the Gracie family was based on jūdō as taught to Carlos Gracie by Mitsuyo Maeda in 1914.

The modern popularisation of mixed martial arts came off the back of the Ultimate Fighting Championship (UFC) in 1993 spearheaded by Rorion Gracie and dominated in the early years by Brazilian jiu jitsu.

Jūdō

Modern jūjutsu is inextricably linked to the development of jūdō.

The older art of jūjutsu, as used by the *samurai*, was developed to maim, kill or capture. A 1892 article from London newspaper The Idler explains the difference between jūjutsu and jūdō: *"The modern school of Ju-Jitsu is now known as the Kōdōkan judo ... The Kanō school adopts this word in preference to 'Ju-Jitsu', for it is not only a physical training, but a moral and intellectual one, the old form, Ju-Jitsu, being solely studied for fighting purposes."*[124]

In modern Japan (after the *Meiji* restoration of 1868), the safety of *uke* took on higher importance to ensure training partners were not injured. *"Dr Kano insisted upon the ethical as well as the purely physical."*[125] Many techniques in jūjutsu and jūdō are the same, but an important distinction is made between the *junte* and the *gyakute* position of the *uke*.

Junte position of the body ensures maximum damage to the opponent and often entangles the limbs so that *ukemi* (break falling) is not possible, or limbs are broken before, or during a throw. The *gyakute* position minimises the risk by angling joints to lower the risk of injury. *"... when a throw is executed correctly with the intention and speed to maim or kill, as was done in fights to the death, taking ukemi was extremely difficult, and the chances of coming out unharmed were slim."*[126]

At the time of jūdō's founder; Jigorō Kanō's (1860-1938) birth, Japan was changing both economically and culturally. The previous generations' feudalism and the ways of the *samurai* class were giving way to a Westernised future of trade and commerce.

Young Japanese men were increasingly unwilling to risk their lives to learn jūjutsu, which, at the time, frequently maimed or killed opponents in contests. Himself a practitioner of jūjutsu styles including: Kito ryū, Tenshin-Shin'yō ryū, Takenouchi ryū and Sosuishitsu ryū jūjutsu, Kanō improved, adapted and codified what he had learned to form jūdō (translated as 'the way of gentleness') in 1882.

---

[124] Burgin, (1892), *The Idler*, p.281
[125] Harrison, (1950), *The Fighting Spirit of Japan*, p.49
[126] Mol, (2001), *Classical Fighting Arts of Japan*, p.22

Kano found it politically necessary to distance himself from the term jūjutsu as, by now it was associated with immorality and outdated ethical principals. The prefix of 'Kodokan' instead of just jūdō was to avoid confusion with the old jūjutsu school of Jikishin ryū jūdō. The 'Kodokan' reference is not entirely clear but Shortt and Hashimoto (1979) have indicated the Kodokan Academy at Mito in Ibaragi province was of liberal pro-western support and representative of modern Japan.[127]

Image 20 – Jigorō Kanō (c1920)

A 1932 extract from Harrison reads:

"Dr. Kano, now a singularly vigorous veteran in his seventies, in his youth made a special study of all the better-known systems (in Japanese 'ryūgi' or sects) of Ju-Jitsu, and after carefully selecting the best that each system had to offer, and rejecting a great deal that was superfluous, he finally elaborated his own eclectic system styled 'judo', which is to-day the one almost universally recognized throughout Japan, where it is taught by Kōdōkan instructors in the Army and Navy, the police, universities and higher schools."[128]

---

[127] Goodger, (1981), The Development of Judo in Britain, p.52
[128] Harrison, (1932), *The Art of Ju-Jitsu*, p.11

Jūdō was developed in a time where battlefield proficiency was no longer a way of testing the student's skills.

Kanō taught through two main training methods; *kata* (forms) and *randori* (sparring). He wanted jūjutsu to be recognised as a modern sport for physical and cultural development, so he excluded the annihilation and deadly techniques from normal practice and from his general syllabus. The 'no-holds-barred' attitude of jūjutsu tournaments were socially unacceptable to the modernising, Westernising Japan and Kanō realised for his Kōdōkan jūdō to survive it needed to be aligned to this new cultural setting.

Kōdōkan jūdō was to have *samurai* traditions mixed with a more modern and Westernised approach.

Kanō built his jūdō on the traditions of ancient Japan, but with an awareness of the future. *Atemi* (striking), and the more dangerous jūjutsu techniques, could be practiced safely in jūdō *kata* (taught at higher-grade level). *Nage-waza* (throwing techniques) and *katame-waza* (grappling techniques) could be practiced through *randori.*

The first jūdō school was founded by Kanō in 1882, the emphasis not just being on physical exercise or technical prowess, but also equally measured with mental discipline and moral virtue. Promoting education, good manners and civilised behavior set jūdō apart from the increasingly disreputable jūjutsu. Kanō took the jū (flexible) and removed the *jitsu* (the art) and replaced with dō (the way) to make a clear distinction for his new system and a different ethical starting point for his students.

Kanō's belt ranking system (discussed further in the ancillary chapter) and his introduction of *randori* - the free-flowing competitive practice were the first two keys to jūdō's success and world-wide popularity, neither of which were present in jūjutsu at the time. The first 'red vs white' contests (*shiai*) began in 1884 and remain to this day the longest-running sporting event in the world.

In 1886 the Tokyo police (*Keishicho*) issued a challenge to Kanō's school. This would be a jūdō vs jūjutsu match to decide upon their adoption of a chosen training method for the police. *"Kanō Ryū stylists won 13 of their matches, lost two and drew one."*[129]

The police favored Kanō's jūdō and placed it in their training regime, making it the official standard of the Japanese government for police and military application. Kanō's practitioners were of the opinion that the older jūjutsu systems were inferior and had begun to drop into disuse. Focus was almost entirely concentrated away from traditional jūjutsu to this new jūdō methodology.

"The Kano system, at the time of its adoption by the Japanese government, consisted of forty-seven tricks of combat and fifteen 'serious' tricks. Additions and amplifications have been made by those great teachers, Hoshino and Tsutsumi, until now the complete system, as we teach it, comprises one hundred and sixty tricks."[130]

Kanō's jūdō was to prioritise the standing techniques and to stop contests transitioning into a more ground-based art. In 1925 Kanō changed the rules to ensure practitioners attained proficiency in standing techniques before taking opponents to the ground. At the inception of jūdō, it is clear Kanō emphasised *randori* and *kata*, physical education and character development as the cornerstones of his art. Its full sporting (Olympic) context would come much later.

By 1942 all sporting versions of jūdō in Japan were shelved in favor of militaristic training to help the Pacific war effort, instructing only those skills relevant to the military. Kanō had died four years earlier. By 1945 the American occupying forces had closed down mass public participation in the martial arts. Having trained Japanese soldiers during the war, the Kōdōkan was closed down by the occupying forces. It reopened some years later after satisfying the occupying powers of its non-militaristic intent. American servicemen, having witnessed and practiced jūdō during the Japanese occupation, took the art home with them and it began to gain popularity in America during the 1950s.

The Japanese were always in favor of open competition without the weight categories which the European (and now international) federations were pushing. Things changed in 1961 when a large Dutchman called Anton Geesink won the world championships. The day after his victory, the Japanese establishment accepted the proposed weight categories and the International Jūdō Federation

---

[129] Shortt, (1979), *Beginning Jiu Jitsu Ryōi-Shinto Style*, p.39
[130] Hancock & Higashi, (1938), *The Complete Kano Jiu Jitsu*, p.x

(IJF) made the change in jūdō's rules. Geesink would go on to win the heavyweight title at the Tokyo Olympics in 1964. The international sporting side of jūdō was gaining more ground over its traditional ethos, and at the same time, was being projected worldwide to an ever-expanding base of new *jūdōka*.

Kanō was a member of the Japanese Olympic Committee, his ideals also aligned with those of Baron Pierre de Coubertin; the founder of the modern Olympic Games. It is debatable to many jūdō traditionalists whether Kanō would have been happy about jūdō appearing as an Olympic sport in 1964 or, more fundamentally, that the sporting version of jūdō was completely overshadowing the other aspects of the art.

Jūdō's popular 'sporting' version introduced and amended its rules continually in response to its competitors, finding more and more loopholes to exploit in competition. Finding a balance between competitors finding new ways to win by points and keeping spectators interested led to a continuing roundabout of rule changes. Jūdō evolved to become more favorable as a spectator sport and safer for its competitors. Significantly, some of the rule changes may have put further limitations on groundwork in competition.

Many of these rule changes to sporting jūdō have not found their way into the traditional grading system. The ethos and spirit for this system remain more closely attached to Kanō's original ideals of jūdō.

"To this day there are many that claim to be experts at judo who know little or nothing beyond the mat craft required to win tournaments. It is unlikely that Kano would have bestowed any great rank upon these people."[131]

The politics of jūdō were beginning to draw two sides, the traditionalists, and the Olympic focused variants of the art. In Britain there was a move to find the official voice of jūdō. In 1963 the British Jūdō Association (BJA), British Jūdō Council (BJC) and Amateur Jūdō Association (AJA) held a contest to decide which authority would have the right to organise the Olympic team. The BJA won and to this day are recognised governmentally as the official voice of jūdō in Britain.

Today, many jūdō clubs and associations concentrate purely on contest jūdō within the limited rules of competition, to the exclusion of many of Kanō's jūjutsu techniques. Jūdō has allowed a large number of practitioners to become full time

---

[131] Hammond, (2008), *Ippon – The Fight for Judo's Soul*, p.9

professionals and to concentrate purely on a competitive sporting version of the original art. Other jūdō clubs still teach *kata* and *atemi* - the uncompetitive aspects of the art which, to some, draws the distinction between 'martial' and 'sporting'.

Jūjutsu students will find their knowledge effectively complements jūdō. Many of the throws are similar, although the emphasis, *kuzushi, junte* and *gyakute* positions and situational concepts can be very different.

Aikidō

Dr Sogaku Takeda's (1859-1943) father was a *samurai* who founded a school of jūjutsu called Daito-ryū Aiki-Jujutsu. One of Takeda's students, Morihei Ueshiba (1883-1969), went on to develop his own style of jūjutsu in the 1920s which he called aikidō.

Image 21 – Morihei Ueshiba (c1950)

With his roots in jūjutsu, Ueshiba, like Kanō, removed the *jutsu* as and replaced it with *dō* symbolising the distinction between a *samurai* warfare art and a more self-cultivating philosophical approach to training.

Like Kanō's jūdō, Ueshiba's aikidō was more concentrated on improving oneself than on destroying the opponent. Aikidō joint locking techniques are designed for takedown and restraint, going with the direction of the opponent's force until it dissipates, rather than aiming primarily to disjoint or injure.

"Do not stare into the eyes of your opponent: he may mesmerise you. Do not fix your gaze on his sword: he may intimidate you. Do not focus on your opponent at all: he may absorb your energy. The essence of the technique is to bring your opponent completely into your sphere. Then you can stand just where you like, in a safe and unassailable position [Ueshiba]."[132]

---

[132] Stevens, (1999), *The Essence of Aikido*, p.114

Uneshiba was said to be a true master of the body and how it moves, he was head professor at Tokyo University in the field of anatomical theory; the study of body movement and muscular bio-structure. Ueshiba also wanted a high degree of spiritual harmony and use of *ki* (that inner, intangible force) to be a fundamental part of his art.

Jūjutsu students will find their knowledge effectively complements aikidō, like jūdō there is a lot of cross-over with jūjutsu.

Ninjutsu

The *ninja* were classical Japanese spies and assassins who tended to work covertly, specialising in espionage, infiltration, assassination and guerilla warfare. The term *shinobi* is more commonly used than *ninja* in Japan. In translation, the word *ninja* has become favored in the West.

Despite the popular view of the *ninja* being anti-*samurai,* this was not always the case. The *ninja* could be working for the same lord as a *samurai* but would be used for different purposes. Where the unarmed martial art of the *samurai* was jūjutsu, the *ninja* would use *ninjutsu* (*shinobi-no-jitsu* and *shinobi jutsu*) to reflect their specialist training. The *ninja* were not bound to the same code of honour (*bushidō*) as the *samurai*, so where a *samurai* might deem a task dishonorable or beneath them, the specialist *ninja* would be used instead.

Where the *samurai* were bred through the noble class, the *ninja* were often recruited from the lower class. Coupled with the fact they operated covertly and were trained on a far smaller scale, there are few historical accounts of them, which helps to add to their mystique. *Ninja* were trained to climb and infiltrate castles and homes undetected to carry out their tasks. The common image of the black-clad *ninja* is not necessarily accurate as the *ninja* would be more commonly dressed as civilians to blend into the crowd and keep their anonymity.

Although the *ninja* were adept with many weapons and tools, like with *samurai* the *katana* was often the primary weapon of choice. However, unlike the *samurai*, the *ninja* would often wear theirs on their backs, to enable them to climb.

Ninjutsu is the martial art of the *ninja*. Although there is no direct translation to English, 'the art of stealth' would be one way of defining the terminology.

The history of *ninjitsu* is very limited, a testament to the professionalism of its practitioners. While many stories and legends of the secret and often superhuman *ninja* exist, the reality is the *ninja* were paid killers using *ninjutsu* to sabotage, assassinate, spy, reconnoitre, raid, burn down and terrorise. These disreputable tasks did not fall under the *samurai's* code of *budō,* which is to say the *ninja* could go where *samurai* would not, and act without conscience, outside of *bushidō.*

Ninjutsu was usually passed on to those 'born into' the profession. The arts and techniques being a closely guarded secret passed from father to son and within a closed *ryū*. Anyone found leaking the secrets could be assassinated by other *ninja*.

The last two practitioners believed to be carrying the full training and range of ancient *ninja* (or *Shinobi*) techniques are:

Jin'ichi Kawakami (1949):
21st Head of the Koga Ban family (Iga and Koga *ninjutsu*)

Masaaki Hatsumi (1931):
34th Grandmaster of the Togakure clan, (three ancient *ninjutsu* and six ancient *samurai* jūjutsu schools)

The need for *ninja* techniques in ancient Japan, and particularly the Edo period (1603-1868), required *ninjas* to be proficient in espionage, assassination and poisoning. Many modern military techniques have had to adapt to technology in the modern world, leaving many ancient ninja techniques and weapons outdated.

Stealth, sabotage and swordsmanship are no longer as effective against automatic weapons, and medical advancements are limiting the effectiveness of traditional *ninja* poison. For this reason, it is believed that neither Kawakami nor Hatsumi will appoint a new grandmaster for their schools.

The last known *ninja* training school in the world is called the *Bujinkan*, headquartered in Japan, and is led by *Sōke* Masaaki Hatsumi who was himself trained by Toshitsugu Takamatsu from a direct line of ancient *ninja*.

Hatsumi's interest in *ninjutsu* came after teaching American GI's jūdō after WWII and realising that their *"drive, power and body dynamism"*[133] allowed them to quickly adapt and apply techniques without the many years of training that he himself had gone through. *"Hatsumi ended his budo training at a moment's notice and started looking again for the roots of the real martial arts, the bujutsu, which he believed could be found deeper down within the Japanese tradition."*[134]

---

[133] Ettig, (2004), *Takamatsu Toshitsugu – The Last Shinobi*, p.135
[134] Ettig, (2004), *Takamatsu Toshitsugu – The Last Shinobi*, p.136

Brazilian Jiu Jitsu

Brazilian jiu jitsu (BJJ) was developed in Brazil by refining existing jūdō and jūjutsu *ne-waza* techniques as well as exploring new methods of groundwork technique.

George Gracie moved from Scotland to Brazil in 1801. One of his grandsons, Gastao, also moved to Brazil after training to be a diplomat in Germany.

Mitsuyo Maeda, a student of Jigorō Kanō's Kōdōkan jūdō, visited Brazil in 1914 and attempted to establish a Japanese colony. Maeda was known to have participated in a string of 'no rules' challenge matches with fighters from all styles. In a chance encounter, Maeda met Gastao Gracie who helped Maeda to settle. In return Meada began to teach Gastao's son, Carlos, the art of jūdō. Carlos Gracie was a dedicated student and devoted himself to this training.

At this time jūdō and jūjutsu were commonly referred to as the same thing. H.J. Harrison visited Japan in 1897 and worked and studied there for over 20 years. He noted in 1950, *"I lived more particularly for the study of the language and the practice of the celebrated art of judo, more commonly known abroad in those days as jujitsu."*[135]

Jūjutsu books of the time, such as Harrison's 1932 pocket guide, refer to jūdō and jūjutsu interchangeably.

Carlos was the oldest of eight children and passed the jūjutsu teachings to his brothers Helio, Oswaldo, Jorge and Gastao. Sometime later the Gracie family moved to Rio de Janerio and Carlos began teaching jiu jitsu to provide an income for the family. The 'Gracie fight challenge' was issued to help establish the credibility of Carlos's teachings.

Helio Gracie was the youngest brother and very frail as a child. Doctors had told him not to participate in physical activity, so he spent his time watching his brothers teach jiu jitsu and observing from the background.

"One day when Helio was sixteen years old, a student showed up for a class with Carlos, who was not there. Helio, who had memorised all the moves of his older brother, offered to start the class, and the student accepted. When the class was over, Carlos showed up and was very apologetic for his delay. The student

---

[135] Harrison, (1950), *The Fighting Spirit of Japan*, p.14

answered, 'No problem. I enjoyed the class with Helio very much. If you don't mind, I'd like to continue having classes with him from now on'."[136]

Helio made it his life's work to pull apart all the jiu jitsu techniques of his brothers and to re-engineer them to suit his weaker physique. In doing so, he increased the leverage of the techniques and reduced the need for strength in their execution.

Like Mitsuyo Maeda and his older brother Carlos, Helio too had an 'open challenge match' approach to his jiu jitsu and in 17 fights was only beaten twice. Once, in 1951 by top judoka Masahiko Kimura, who outweighed him by 35kg, and once in 1955 by his own student Valdemar Santana, who was 16 years his junior.

In Helio's 2005 book, 'Gracie Jiu-Jitsu,' he says of the Kimura fight, *"From the moment he stepped into the ring, Helio felt as if he was shoved inside a blender."*[137]

Image 22 – Masahiko Kimura and Helio Gracie (1951)

---

[136] Gracie, (2005), *Gracie Jiu-Jitsu*, p.2
[137] Gracie, (2005), *Gracie Jiu-Jitsu*, p.4

The Valdemar Santana fight lasted three hours and forty minutes and ended with Helio knocked out from a kick to the head. Later that year, when Carlson Gracie drew Santana in a rematch to avenge his uncle, the rules were adjusted to suit jiu jitsu as opposed to raw *vale tudo* as the first fight with Helio had been so savage. The crowds preferred the *vale tudo* style and a second rematch took place in 1956, with Carlson winning by technical knockout nine minutes into the fourth round.

Image 23 – Valdemar Santana (left) vs Helio Gracie (1956)

Helio's eldest son, Rorion Gracie, took the redesigned jiu jitsu to Los Angeles and began teaching from the garage at his rented house[138]. Richard Bresler was Rorion's first American student[139]. Rorion's brother, Royce, joined him to help teach the new style they called 'Gracie Jiu-Jitsu'. By 1989 the garage was so busy that Rorion and his brothers Rickson, Royler and Royce were able to open the Gracie academy in Torrance California.

By 1993 Rorion had developed the concept for 'The Ultimate Fighting Championship' (UFC) and, rather than Rickson, who was the family champion, Royce was chosen to represent Gracie jiu jitsu as he was smaller and less intimidating. It would make for a greater spectacle and a more convincing portrayal of the art when he took down and beat the larger opponents.

---

[138] Bresler (2021), *Worth Defending*
[139] Bresler (2021), *Worth Defending*

Royce Gracie won the first Ultimate Fighting Championship in 1993 and today no fighter entering such a competition does so without techniques from Brazilian jiu jitsu.

There are four disciplines in Brazilian Jiu Jitsu as noted in Table 14, Gi, no Gi, MMA and self defence.

Brazilian jiu jitsu has followed a similar path to jūdō in the respect that champions of the sporting aspect of the art have inspired more students to concentrate solely on this aspect. Like jūdō before it, Brazilian jiu jitsu has formed two distinct sides, sporting, and martial. The sporting side appeals more to the masses and has greater financial motivations.

Figure 25 – Passing the guard in Brazilian Jiu Jitsu

Jūjutsu in Mixed Martial Arts

When observing jūjutsu in mixed martial arts competition, as violent and skillful as this sport is, it is just that, a sport. The *samurai* had no referee, no time limits on the battlefield, and the difference between winning and losing was, more often than not, life or death. Mixed Martial Arts (MMA) is a hybrid of techniques from both martial arts and ring sports. Practitioners rarely study 'traditional' jūjutsu as it would contradict the aims of the sport.

For MMA, jūjutsu displays a limited range of techniques. However, the essence of this contested free practice hones the practitioner's skills in these particular techniques far more than could ever be achieved through compliant practice. MMA also proves the effectiveness of the jūjutsu techniques it uses by demonstrating them against an opponent who is consequently thrown or subdued.

These 'no-holds-barred' matches have shown the effectiveness of jūjutsu through the elimination of poor technique proven to be ineffective in such a fight. Today's MMA fighters have learned to only train in those techniques that work within the rules of the sport.

Flying kicks and rigid classical blocks are of no use against a trained opponent. Successful fighters have a core base of Brazilian jiu jitsu groundwork, wrestling takedowns and clinch work, muay thai kicks, knee and elbow strikes, boxing punches and (above all), a high level of fitness, conditioning and flexibility.

MMA has in fact taken all the fit-for-purpose techniques from all martial arts proven within the rules of the sport, and created a very effective mix of techniques that have been pressure tested and proven to function against real resistance. This was predicted to some degree by Bankier who stated in 1905, having just been introduced to jūjutsu; *"I believe that if a man knew a little of boxing, and had, moreover, a knowledge of Japanese wrestling, he would be a dangerous man to tackle, no matter what his weight."* [140]

In jūjutsu there is often debate about the effectiveness of techniques 'diluted' by sport vs their martial applications. The annihilation and mutilation techniques of jūjutsu, such as groin strikes and eye gouges, cannot be practiced outside of life-

---

[140] Bankier, (1905), *Ju-Jitsu, What it Really Is*, p.39

and-death scenarios. Nevertheless, training can still take place with a cooperative *uke*.

Too much sparring under limited rules can also bring about problems when faced with a 'real' scenarios, striking to the forehead, for example, as when used to wearing gloves, can often result in a broken hand which may have consequences for the remainder of the encounter. Striking to the face can also damage the hand when making contact with teeth, and cross-contamination with blood carries the risk of serious infection. Jūjutsu palm heel strikes or slaps would be more useful in this scenario but would not be trained by the MMA fighter, who would have no use for them.

MMA does not use weapons or defend from them or from multiple attackers, all very real possibilities in a self-defence situation. However, the vigorous practice allowed by MMA and competition (much as used in jūdō and BJJ) is essential for the modern *jūjutsuka* to reach their full pressure-tested potential.

The 'best' martial art is to have no martial art. This means melting anatomical knowledge and all martial arts techniques into a physical encyclopedia of muscle memory that can blend and flow with only a personal style. This concept was realised by Bruce Lee and in his book, *The TAO of Jeet Kune Do* he states: *"If people say Jeet Kune Do is different from 'this' or from 'that' then let the name of Jeet Kune Do be wiped out. For that is what it is, just a name, please don't fuss over it."*[141]

---

[141] Lee, (1975), *The Tao of Jeet Kune Do*, p.208

Chapter 6: Ancillary

その他

The Uniform of Jūjutsu

There are reasons for the design of the jūjutsu uniform, just as there are for all those seemingly unexplainable military dress uniforms found in armed forces across the world. Generally the reasoning behind such uniforms pays homage to the past.

Modern jūjutsu is practiced in *keikogi*. The translation from Japanese to English would be *keiko* meaning 'practice' and *gi* meaning 'clothes'. *Keikogi* would be common to most Japanese martial arts from the 1920s onwards. Before this time, everyday clothes would be used for practicing martial arts.

The *gi* as it is now commonly referred to, is often incorrectly termed as *kimono*. The *kimono* dates back to Japan's Heian period (794-1192) and is a T-shaped, straight-lined robe. It was often worn with the *hakama* (a divided trouser skirt) over the top. In some styles of jūjutsu today you will see the *hakama* worn over the *keikogi*; this is often used for rank identification. Jūjutsu masters began to wear the *hakama* to disguise the intricacies of leg positioning and movement therefore keeping their school's secrets to those whom only they chose to teach.

During the Japanese Muromachi period (1392-1573) the *kimono* began to be worn without the *hakama*, and the top was closed by use of the *obi* (a belt). During the Edo period (1603-1868) the *kimono* sleeves began to get longer and the belt wider, the *kimono* of the Edo period has remained unchanged to this day. As pre-1920s jūjutsu was practiced in everyday clothes, a *kimono* would have been common for martial arts practice but not designed specifically for this purpose. The *kimono* is always fastened with the left-hand side over the right and today's jūjutsu *gi* are tied in exactly the same way. Right over left is reserved for funerary purposes.

Today's *keikogi* was developed by jūdō founder, Jigorō Kanō, around 1920. The heavy jacket (*uwagi*) would withstand the rigors of being pulled and stretched during practice. The founder of shotokan karate, Gichin Funakoshi, was among the first to adopt the *keikogi* for training and later adapted it to a lighter fabric more suited to karate.

Modern jūjutsu also followed jūdō in adopting the *keikogi* for training. The *jūjutsugi* in use today consists of *uwagi* (jacket) and *shitabaki* (trousers) with a coloured *obi* (belt) to represent rank.

The *jūjutsigi* is generally available in four thicknesses. These materials are common to jūjutsu, BJJ and jūdō uniforms and are shown in Table 23.

Table 23 – Types of uniform (gi) material

Single weave	A lighter material for training and summer use
Double weave	A heavy thick material for competition use
Gold weave	In between single and double weave
Platinum weave	A lighter version of the gold weave

Jūdō was practiced in a white *jodogi* and jūjutsu in a white or black *jūjutsigi*. In the 1980s jūdō adopted the blue coloured *gi* to make it easier for spectators to distinguish between competitors. During the 1990s the rise of BJJ in MMA competitions led to an explosion of multicoloured gi's which have filtered back for use in jūjutsu.

Modern jūjutsu cubs tend to train in a mix of *gi* as well as sportswear, which can be advantageous for self-defence training as it mimics today's reality on the street much like the *kimono* did in classical jūjutsu training.

The Belt Ranking System

The coloured belt ranking system came after the practicality of needing a belt to secure the uniform *uwagi* (jacket). Today in jūjutsu there are a range of coloured belts (usually around seven) which are referred to as the *kyū* grades, and ten levels of black belt which are referred to as the *dan* grades.

Ranked belts in *samurai* times were unnecessary as their *bushidō* code had no reason to distinguish between levels of skill in unarmed combat, this could easily be settled by competition or battle.

During the Meiji period (1868-1912) when Japan was westernising and jūjutsu had to go underground, knowledge was passed on and kept secret within rival *ryū*. Again, the belt system was not yet in use. Recognition was often passed on in *makimono* with the secrets of the particular school inscribed.

Koryu based warrior training systems (794-1868) do not award belts. A *menkyo* (certificate) in the style is instead awarded, one for each aspect of training similar to Table 3. When a student had passed the entire curriculum they would be awarded a *menkyo kaiden*, the license of total transmission and quite possibly *makimono* with the schools secrets inscribed.

Tabizayemon Yamamoto (c1550) who was a master of the Yoshin ryū, founded his own jūjutsu school called Shin-no-shindo ryū. The techniques were *"classified into shodan (preliminary rank); chudan (middle rank), and jodan (upper rank)."*[142] This may have been the first organised differentiation of rank (or belt).

Modern Jūjutsu Grading System

Much like the *keikogi*, the modern belt ranking system was developed by jūdō founder Jigorō Kanō in 1886. At this time, the only differentiation was that senior students wore a black *obi* over their *uwagi*. In 1907 Kanō introduced the white belt to contrast with the existing black belt, and at the time these were the only two ranks available. In around 1930 Kanō introduced the alternating red-and-white belt (*kohaku obi*) to further recognise high ranking black-belt students. The optional red belt was introduced in 1943 to recognise 9th and 10th dan grades.

---

[142] Harrison, (1932), *The Art of Ju-Jitsu*, p.17

Mikinosuke Kawaishi (Image 15 page 60) is generally recognised as being the first person to define the coloured belt system for the *kyū* grades. Again, jūdō is credited for this. Kawaishi started the system in 1935 after realising his students in Paris responded better to the visible recognition of progress. The jūdō uniform and belt ranking system were eventually adopted by other martial arts, including modern jūjutsu.

There is no worldwide acceptance in the order of coloured jūjutsu grades, just a general recognition that the black belt symbolises that one has learnt all the basics of the art and can now progress and teach others as well as personalising what they have learned so far.

Table 24 – Typical modern jūjutsu belt ranking system

Belt	Grade	Japanese Term
White	7th *Kyū*	*Mukyū*
Yellow	6th *Kyū*	*Rokkyū*
Orange	5th *Kyū*	*Gokyū*
Green	4th *Kyū*	*Yonkyū*
Blue	3rd *Kyū*	*Sankyū*
Purple	2nd *Kyū*	*Nikyū*
Brown	1st *Kyū*	*Ikkyū*
Black	*Dan*	*Shodan – Ho*
Black	1st *Dan*	*Shodan*
Black	2nd *Dan*	*Nidan*
Black	3rd *Dan*	*Sandan*
Black	4th *Dan*	*Yondan*
Black	5th *Dan*	*Godan*
Red and White	6th *Dan*	*Rokudan*
Red and White	7th *Dan*	*Shichidan*
Red and White	8th *Dan*	*Hachidan*
Red	9th *Dan*	*Kudan*
Red	10th *Dan*	*Jūdan*

Kyū means 'class' and *dan* means 'step'. The modern system is referred to as the *dan* system; older systems are referred to as *menkyo* systems.

The modern system can look like organised complexity in comparison with older *menkyo* systems; this is because belts were not needed in ancient Japan, as survival in combat was all the qualification needed. The modern system caters for a part-time student who can be kept motivated and have a visual sign of progress through their training. It is also an easy, visual way to identify students who can practice the more dangerous techniques based on their experience level.

As well as the belt ranking system, various titles (often grade related) can be bestowed upon practitioners to signify positions within the club or association.

Table 25 – Modern jūjutsu rank titles

Sōke	Head of style
Hanshi	Professor, senior expert, teacher of teachers, grandmaster
Kyōshi	Assistant professor or advanced teacher
Shihan	Chief or senior instructor
Renshi	Polished expert
Sensei	Teacher
Yūdansha	Black belt
Senpai	Senior *kyū* grade or assistant teacher
Mudansha	*Kyū* belt grade
Mon	Junior grade (translated as 'gate')

Sōke is a title reserved for the head of a martial arts family; this is often dependent on the size of that family. *Sōke* are often mistakenly referred to as the founders of styles (as a lot of *sōke* are founders as well), but the title can also be passed on. A *sōke* is considered to be the ultimate authority within their jūjutsu style.

Hanshi is reserved for the top few instructors of a style. Often referred to as 'grandmasters' in English, *hanshi* are more than just practitioners of the art: they have political and innovative involvement. *Hanshi* is generally 8th dan and above.

Kyōshi is a special status in jūjutsu in which you are able to teach the philosophy of the art and not just the practical application. *Kyōshi* is usually 7th dan and above.

Shihan is an expert or senior instructor with many years' experience. *Shihan* is often conferred with certain rights, such as awarding senior *dan* grades. Promotion to *shihan* is often said to occur when other *shihan* start calling you *shihan*. This is usually 6th *dan* and above.

Renshi is reserved for an expert in the art, often in practical application and instruction. *Renshi* is generally awarded to selected practitioners of the modern rank of 4th *dan* and above.

The *sensei* title is earned and officially awarded, not necessarily a given title for a black belt. The *sensei* has a responsibility to pass on their knowledge of jūjutsu to the next generation. With this passing of knowledge, the *sensei* themself becomes better, and so their development in jūjutsu is somewhat tied to their experience as a teacher.

Senpai is not an assumed title at a certain grade level, but an awarded title from the *sensei* to senior *kyū* grade students who display a discipline and willingness that represent the dedication the *sensei* is looking for.

The term *shodan* can be broken down and translated as follows: *sho* meaning '1st' and *dan* meaning 'man' in Japanese. Traditionally, a junior (*mon*) graded student could not become *shodan* until they were aged 16, as they were not felt mature enough to achieve the black belt until then.

It is often thought by those outside the martial arts that the gaining of a 'black belt' makes one an expert and master of the art. In reality, the black belt is only the start of the journey. It signifies that one has learnt all the basics and only then can begin to fully appreciate what they have been taught and pass their knowledge on to others.

It is common in many jūjutsu schools to be graded against a set syllabus up to and including *sandan* (3rd *dan*). Thereafter, grades (form certain schools) can be awarded by merit, usually by a panel of senior grades.

Brazilian Jiu Jitsu Grading System

Where modern jūjutsu gradings rely more on a pre-set syllabus of techniques to achieve the next grade it is more common in BJJ to demonstrate an ability to cope in various scenarios, not necessarily on being able to perform a pre-set number of specific techniques.

The white, blue, purple and brown grades have up to four 'degrees' on each belt which are indicated by white stripes.

Table 26 – Brazilian Jiu Jitsu belt ranking system

White	1st to 4th Degree
Blue	1st to 4th Degree
Purple	1st to 4th Degree
Brown	1st to 4th Degree
Black	1st Degree
Black	2nd Degree
Black	3rd Degree
Black	4th Degree
Black	5th Degree
Black	6th Degree
Red & Black (Coral)	7th Degree
Red & White (Coral)	8th Degree
Red	9th Degree
Red	10th Degree

Black belts are addressed as 'professor' or 'coach'.

The earliest age for 9th degree belt (according to the IBJJF) is 67 years old. The 10th Dan is reserved for the founding Gracie brothers.

The white belt is about survival, being constantly tapped out by the higher belts, learning how to move into and out of the different positions and working towards a well-rounded skill set of basic offensive moves such as submissions and passes.

The blue belt is a learning of technical knowledge, students get proficient at gaining positional advantage, escaping from non-dominant positions and being able to execute submissions.

The purple belt is where the student has gained a highly proficient level of technique and is capable of helping to train others at the lower belts

The brown belt is where the student refines the techniques they have learned and goes on to develop their own personal style and preference.

The black belt is an expert level of technical and practical skill.

Jūdō Grading System

Where modern jūjutsu belt ranking systems can differ between different organisations, jūdō is internationally codified by governing bodies such as the International Judo Federation (IJF), Kodokan Judo Institute and the World Judo Federation (WJF).

There is common agreement on the belt structure and colour from 1st *Dan* and above, but the *kyū* grade colours and progression varies between associations and countries.

Table 27 – British Judo Association (BJA) Kyū grades

Belt	Grade
White	Novice
Red	6th *Kyū*
Yellow	5th *Kyū*
Orange	4th *Kyū*
Green	3rd *Kyū*
Blue	2nd *Kyū*
Brown	1st *Kyū*

Table 28 – Internationally recognised jūdō Dan grades

Belt	Grade	Japanese Term
Black	1st *Dan*	*Shodan*
Black	2nd *Dan*	*Nidan*
Black	3rd *Dan*	*Sandan*
Black	4th *Dan*	*Yondan*
Black	5th *Dan*	*Godan*
Red and White	6th *Dan*	*Rokudan*
Red and White	7th *Dan*	*Shichidan*
Red and White	8th *Dan*	*Hachidan*
Red	9th *Dan*	*Kudan*
Red	10th *Dan*	*Jūdan*

Jūdō set the standard for coloured belt systems, jūjutsu and Brazilian jiu jitsu followed suit but with their own interpretations. The thing that remains consistent across almost all martial arts is the White belt being the start point and the Black belt being the expert level.

Jūjutsu Syllabus

The techniques shown in Table 29 highlight a typical white-to-black modern jūjutsu or *gaijin goshin* jūjutsu core syllabus. Schools vary greatly, so 'typical' is somewhat misleading. Often, each technique is expected to be performed on both the right- and left-hand sides.

Syllabus techniques are sub-divided down into belts (not shown) to enable the student to progress in smaller, more manageable sections with the motivation of a different coloured belt at the end of each section and the pressure of a 'grading' (test) to pass each belt.

Each technique is expected to be performed from an increasing variation of start points as progression through the belts is made. To begin, students will follow a pre-scripted version of each technique.

Ultimately, the black belt should be able to flow seamlessly (often both right- and left-handed) from one technique to another without hesitation or thought, reacting instinctively on muscle-memory based on the unique situation at that point in time.

Table 29 – Typical example of a full modern (gaijin goshin) jūjutsu syllabus

Throws		
Hip Throws:	Hip throw	*O-goshi*
	Sweeping loin	*Harai-goshi*
	Stamp throw	
	Loin wheel	*Koshi-guruma*
	Spring hip	*Hane-goshi*
Body Drops:	Body drop	*Tai-otoshi*
	Dropping version	
	Advanced dropping version	
	Dropping reverse	
	Cross ankle	
Shoulder Throws:	Half shoulder	*Ippon-seoi-nage*
	Full shoulder	*Seio-nage*
	Dropping full shoulder	*Seoi-otoshi*
	Shoulder wheel	*Kata-guruma*
Sacrifice Throws:	Recumbent ankle	
	Crab claw scissors	*Kani-basami*
	Rice bale	*Tawara-gaeshi*
	Front scissors	
	Valley drop	*Tani-otoshi*
	Rear throw	
	Corner throw	*Sumi-gaeshi*
	Rolling ankle	
	Stomach throw	*Tomoe-nage*
Leg Throws:	Leg throw with lock	
	Drawing ankle	*Deashi-barai*
	Knee wheel	
	Leg wheel	*Ashi-guruma*
	Outer wheel	
Hock Throws:	Inside hock	
	Cross hock	
Scoop Throws:	Front scoop	*Sukui-nage*
	Rear scoop	

Winding Throws:	Outer winding	Soto-makikomi
	Inner winding	
Other Throws:	Wrist throw	
	Head hip and knee	Uki-otoshi
	Arm and shoulder	

Locks	Escapes
Straight arm lock	Escapes from front strangles
Shoulder lock	Escapes from back strangles
Cross over arm lock	Escape when held over/under the arms, front & rear
Arm locks from a standing position	Escapes from head chancery
Shoulder arm lock (+ advanced)	
Wrist locks from a push	Escapes from half nelsons
Hold down double arm lock	Escape from full nelson
Back hammer lock	Escape when both hands are held from behind
Indian death lock	**Breakfalls**
Blocks	Rolling
Rising	Front and back
Downward	Side
Cross	Flip over
Inside	**Defences / Counters**
Outside	Defences against kicks whilst on the ground
Use of x block with follow up	Breaks from wrist grabs
Strikes	Counters to garrotting
Palm heel	Defence against attacker with swinging chain
Knife hand	Counters to straight arm locks
Ridge hand	Counters to back arm and collar holds
Elbow	Counters to a bar choke
Open hand	**Ground Work**
Bottom fist	Breaks from ground strangles
Kicks	Hold down katas
Front	**Chokes**
Side	Bar choke
	Scissors naked choke

Roundhouse	Sleeper hold from head chancery
Kata	**Weapons**
Strangles and chokes	Defence against knife attacks
Atemi-waza	*Jō Kata*
Hold down	**Other**
Blocks	Etiquette
	Resuscitation and first aid
	Knowledge of nerve and pressure points

Figure 26 – Jūjutsu stomach throw – tomoe-nage

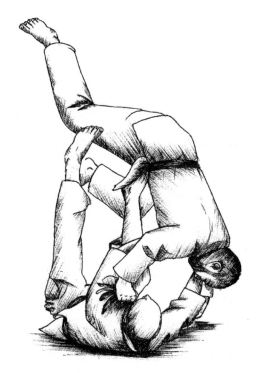

The Weapons of Jūjutsu

Jūjutsu is not a weaponless art. Some modern schools, especially those teaching modern self-defence, do not include the use of weapons (most would be considered illegal to carry today) but historically they have been used in conjunction with jūjutsu to supplement its effectiveness in combat. Jūjutsu can be used for three main purposes:

Table 30 - Uses of jūjutsu

1.	Body-to-body unarmed combat
2.	A way to position the opponent in preparation for using a weapon
3.	Whilst using a weapon closely associated with jūjutsu

The rigorous discipline, technical and psychological training of the *samurai* enabled them to confront their enemies without fear, being in full control of themselves and the situation. The armed *bu-jutsu* (weapons techniques) of the *samurai* included war fans, staffs, *jitte,* sickle and chains, *tonfa*, clubs and *nunchaku* with archery, spear fighting and swordsmanship representing the three major arts. Unlike *budō, bujutsu* trained the warrior in the use of his weapons through actual combat.

This chapter outlines some of the main weapons of classical (794-1868) jūjutsu. There is a wealth of information on each item as an individual study to be found elsewhere.

Sword

The *samurai* carried two swords. Two swords worn together are known as a *daishō* and represented the *samurai's* position in Japanese society. Which of the two (sized) swords were chosen varied depending on the time and intended use.

The *tachi* and *daitō* were worn on the hip, blade facing downwards. The *tachi* was predominantly for use on horseback when the sword was drawn and then brought back down from a height.

The *katana* was lighter than the *tachi* and worn blade upwards. It could be used more quickly, being effective from the moment it was drawn. The *wakizashi* was shorter still and more useful in confined environments such as houses or castles. It was also used for beheading an enemy or for ritual suicide.

Custom dictated the *daishō* to be separated in the home or within the ruling lord's palace. The *tachi* or *katana* would be left at the entrance, but the *wakizashi* would be more consistently kept by the *samurai's* side.

The art of drawing the sword is called *iaido*, and there are many martial arts schools who practice this. The sword is a symbolisation of Japan and there are substantial rules of etiquette associated with its use.

The art of sword fighting is called *ken-jutsu* which *"… became highly specialised, and many schools (ryū) were established where the devotees of the skill, trained assiduously for long hours, practising the initial preparation for combat, the unsheathing of the sword, strategies of attack, counter-attack, and defence."*[143]

Figure 27 – Japanese swords by length

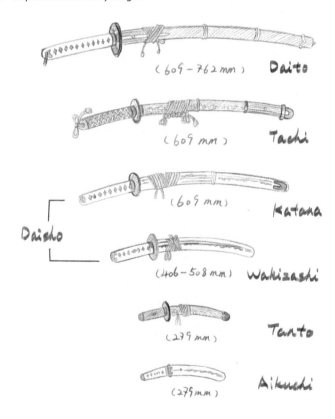

---

[143] Clark & Morris, (1985), *Samurai Budo*.

Table 31 – Types of Japanese sword and approximate lengths

Daitō	609 to 762mm
Tachi	609mm
Katana	609mm
Wakizashi	508 to 406mm
Tantō	279mm
Aikuchi	279mm

There are entire books devoted to the history, construction, etiquette, training and use of the Japanese sword. To the *samurai*, jūjutsu and *kenjutsu* would have been trained simultaneously. The modern martial art of sword practice is called *kendō*.

As Gluck (1973) writes of the famous Japanese Swordsman Musashi Minamoto:

"During his early days in that southernmost of Japan's four main islands, he learned European fencing, including the use of two rapiers, from the Dutch, English and Portuguese around Nagasaki. This skill he wedded to the Japanese weapon – or weapons, for the Japanese had for centuries carried two swords; one, a two-handed sword with a blade of about 3 ft and the other a single-hander of between one and two feet, each with its own separate use. The result was the Musashi two-sword style."[144]

Image 24 – Miyamoto Musashi (c1584-1645)

---

[144] Gluck, (1973), *Zen Combat*, p.89

Bokken

The use of the sword in Japan often ended up in duels which frequently resulted in loss of life. Between legislation and the need to practice safely, the wooden *bokutō* or *bokken* would be used in place of steel. In the hands of an expert the *bokken* can be as lethal as the *katana* or *wakizashi*.

"The most famous of all Japanese swordsmen [Musashi] preffered the bokken, or wooden sword, in combat simply because it was indestructible."[145]

Figure 28 - Bokken

Knife

The Japanese knife (depending upon its length) is called a *tantō*. After grappling in armour a *samurai* would use a knife called a *yoroi-doshi* to penetrate the weak spots in enemy armour.

Knife attacks are becoming increasing common in modern society, and so knife use is as relevant today as it was in the times of ancient Japan.

Major W.E. Fairbairn sums up knife fighting in his 1942 hand-to-hand combat guide; *"In close-quarters fighting, there is no more deadly weapon than the knife. An entirely unarmed man has no certain defence against it, and, further, merely the sudden flashing of a knife is frequently enough to strike fear into your opponent, causing him to lose confidence and surrender."*[146]

The defensive techniques taught in jūjutsu are the same as they were in ancient Japan. A knife was just a knife even 1,000 years ago, so the techniques are as valid today as they were then. The aim is to disarm the opponent as quickly as possible with the least risk to oneself and others and then control or dispose of the knife whilst controlling or incapacitating the opponent.

---

[145] Draeger, (1973), *Classical Bujutsu*, p.56
[146] Fairbairn, (1924), *Get Tough! How to win in hand-to-hand fighting*, p.96

Figure 29 - Knife

The untrained knife-wielding attacker has a limited range of attacks which can be specifically trained for. A trained assailant with a knife is very difficult to disarm open-handed.

Stick

There are three sizes of stick:

Table 32 - Names and sizes of stick weapons

Bō	1,829mm
Jō	1,219mm
Hanbō	914mm
Baton / short stick	< 304mm

Figure 30 – Stick names by length

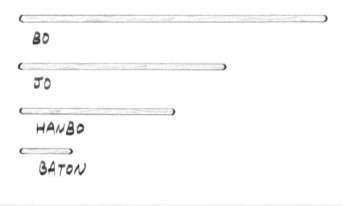

The *samurai* used wooden weapons to train techniques, which in actual combat would involve a steel blade. The wooden staff would often be a training substitute for a spear although the techniques worked equally well with either. Wooden weapons are commonly used in today's *ryū* as they are both practical and realistic and could be used after Japan's edict forbidding the wearing of swords.

The art of using the long stick is called *jō-jutsu* and traces its origins back to a famous swordsman called Gonnosuke Musō who practised the art of the *jō* after losing a bout to the famous swordsman, Musashi Miyamoto. Gonnosuke perfected 12 basic blows and blocks which he later combined into the basis of modern *jōdō* with more than 70 techniques practised through *kata*.

Spear

Long spears, known as *yari*, were used by the warrior monks (*sōhei*) of ancient Japan who could be called upon to fight for the Emperor. The *yari* was 5,486mm (6 yards) long. Nobunaga Oda, a young *daimyō* started to train his army in the use of shorter *yari* 2,438mm (8ft) during his campaign to overthrow the Emperor. Oda did not see the end of his campaign, but one of his generals, Lyeasu Tokugawa, did, starting off the Edo / Tokugawa period of Japan. The art of using the *yari* was called *so-jutsu* and exponents were so proficient by the end of the feudal period in 1867 that many swordsmen were intimidated by these spearmen.

Figure 31 - Naginata

Techniques of the *yari* and *naginata* (curved bladed spear) exist today, but most commonly in jūjutsu the student will find their teachings in the similar weapons of the *jo* and *jo-jutsu*.

Chain
The *kusari* (chain) was used to immobilise an opponent's arms and for strangulation, wrapping around the ankles for a takedown, stretching out to parry a sword or striking with a weighted end for a deadly blow. A chain attached to a short stick is called a *kusari-gama*. Although you would not find a chain on the modern battlefield, the effectiveness of the chain is still deadly in a street fight or mugging, and a lot of *goshin* jūjutsu syllabuses will include defences from a swinging or strangling chain.

Figure 32 - Kusari

Kama

Primarily a farming tool, the *kama* was adapted for fighting and came into the Japanese combative arsenal. Its similarity with the mace or axe found all over the world is apparent. The *kama* was most commonly associated with the *yamabushi* warrior monks, who were extremely proficient in its use.

Figure 33 - Kama

Jitte

Variations of the *jitte* (or *sai*) appear all over the world as a parrying weapon of various designs, with at least one sharp point or with a blade. In Japan, the *jitte* was effective for parrying and trapping a sword, giving the defender time to strike with a point if using two *jitte* in combination with each other.

Figure 34 – Types of Jitte

Tonfa

A versatile, traditional weapon which can be used singularly or in pairs, offensive or defensive. The *tonfa* was adapted by farmers from their tools for cultivation, originally a tool for the grinding and polishing of rice.

Figure 35 - Tonfa

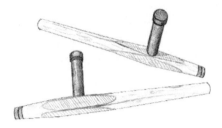

Nunchaku

Like the *tonfa*, the *nunchaku* was adapted from farming implements used to separate grain.

Figure 36 - Nunchaku

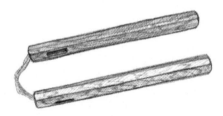

Hōjō Jutsu

Hōjō jutsu (or *Hōjō waza*) involves using a *hojō* cord (a small length of cord or rope) to restrain an attacker. These techniques have largely been replaced with modern handcuffs, but approximately 133 rope techniques are still being taught by specialist instructors.

Grappling in full armour was known as *yoroi kumi-uchi*; *"The warriors closed range and grappled with each other whilst trying to drive a special blade known as a yorio-doshi through joints in the armour. Hōjō Jutsu, the 'techniques of tying' went hand in glove with yorio kumi-uchi. These used the cord that each warrior carried, to single-handedly bind the struggling opponent."*[147]

Smaller, Concealed or Secret Weapons

Small weapons (*kobuki*), hidden weapons (*kakushibuki*) and secret weapons (*hibuki*) are all used in jūjutsu.

---

[147] Clark, (1988), *Masters' Jiu Jitsu*, p.16

These weapons were mainly developed in the Edo / Tokugawa period (1603-1868) for street fighting (without armour) and were often designed and bespoke to a particular school or individual. This type of weapon was used to strike *atemi* (vital) parts of the body.

Figure 37 – Types of tekken

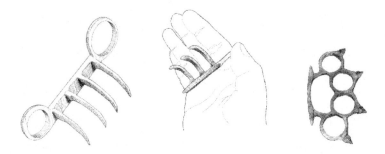

Figure 38 – Iron fan

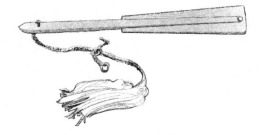

Figure 39 – Types of kubotan

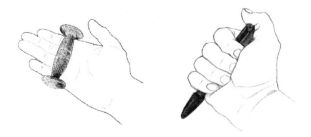

Figure 40 – Kakute and tenouchi

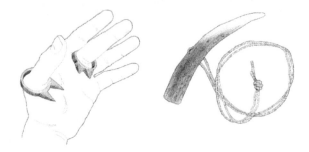

Figure 41 – Suntetsu and fundokusari

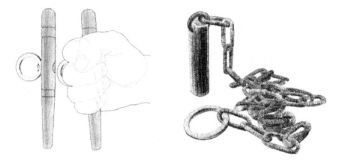

Self-defence and UK Law

UK law is updated regularly by statutes and common law therefore this chapter is only intended as a brief summary in order to grasp the main concepts.

Statute Law[148]
A 'statute' is a law that has been passed through parliament, often referred to as statute law.

Section 3 of the Criminal Law Act 1967 states: *"A person may use such force as is reasonable in the circumstances in the prevention of crime, or in effecting or assisting in the lawful arrest of offenders or suspected offenders or of persons lawfully at large"*

Common Law[149]
Common law is based on the outcomes of previous similar legal cases, where a decision is made it forms a 'precedent' which other cases can follow, some precedents are as old as the law itself.

The basic principles of self-defence are set out in Palmer v R, [1971] AC 814; approved in R v McInnes, 55 Cr App R 551: *"It is both good law and good sense that a man who is attacked may defend himself. It is both good law and good sense that he may do, but only do, what is reasonably necessary."*

Reasonable Force[150]
A person may use such force as is 'reasonable' in the circumstances for the purposes of: self-defence, defence of another, defence of property, prevention of crime, or lawful arrest.

---

[148] Crown Prosecution Service (CPS) www.cps.gov.uk.
[149] Crown Prosecution Service (CPS) www.cps.gov.uk.
[150] Crown Prosecution Service (CPS) www.cps.gov.uk.

Subjectively, the person applying the force must ask themselves two questions:

(1) was the use of force necessary in the circumstances?, and

(2) was the force used reasonable in the circumstances?

The jury must then go on to ask themselves whether, on the basis of the facts as the accused believed them to be, a reasonable person would regard the force used as necessary or reasonable ?

"If there has been an attack so that self defence is reasonably necessary, it will be recognised that a person defending himself cannot weigh to a nicety the exact measure of his defensive action. If the jury thought that that in a moment of unexpected anguish a person attacked had only done what he honestly and instinctively thought necessary, that would be the most potent evidence that only reasonable defensive action had been taken ..." (Palmer v R 1971 AC 814).

Pre-emptive Strikes[151]
There is no rule in law to say that a person must wait to be struck first before they may defend themselves, *cited in* R v Deana, 2 Cr App R 75. Clearly it would be more difficult to prove self-defence in court if a pre-emptive strike was used.

Training Consequences
The person defending themselves has limited time to make a decision, often the trained *jūjutsuka* may react on instinct and muscle memory, this is why; how and what, you do in training can affect your reaction on the street. For example it is bad practice in training, when doing knife defences to stab *uke* after disarming them, this would generally be considered unnecessary and unreasonable force and would therefore be illegal so it should not be programmed into the students muscle memory.

---

[151] Crown Prosecution Service (CPS) www.cps.gov.uk.

Jūjutsu Black Belt (Shodan) Theory Test

Shodan is understandably a test of the *jūjutsuka's* ability to perform (and often teach) the fundamentals of jūjutsu according to the school's particular syllabus. The following questions are designed to complement that practical examination by establishing a baseline of knowledge around the wider concepts of jūjutsu.

Brown belt students, on receiving a copy of this book, should be encouraged to read for the answers and then complete the theory test under exam conditions.

Q1 – What is the generic Japanese term for a student who has achieved Black Belt or above?
a) Shodan
b) Yūdansha
c) Mudansha
d) Renshi

Q2 – In what period of ancient Japan was the 'golden age' of jūjutsu?
a) Meiji Restoration
b) Shōwa Period
c) Edo period
d) Ancient Period

Q3 – The moral code of the samurai is known as:
a) Buddhism
b) Bushidō
c) Mukso
d) Rei

Q4 - What is the Japanese terminology for 'throwing techniques'?
a) Ukemi-waza
b) Atemi-waza
c) Nage-waza
d) Ne-waza

Q5 – Self defence is legal in the uk if used with:

a) Caution

b) Tantō

c) A witness

d) Reasonable force

Q6 – How many named bones are there in the human body?

a) 206

b) 156

c) 260

d) 203

Q7 – Who invented jūjutsu and used it on the battlefield?

a) Jigarō Kanō

b) The Samurai

c) Kajima and Kadori

d) Tabizaemon Yamamoto

Q8 – Jūjutsu translates in English as:

a) Science of combat

b) Art of fighting

c) The gentle art

d) Way of suppleness

Q9 – Who did the samurai fight for?

a) The Shōgun

b) The Rōnin

c) The Sensei

d) The Sōke

Q10 – Which scientist first defined the principle of leverage?

a) Newton

b) Einstein

c) Archimedes

d) Da Vinci

Q11 – What is Newton's 2nd law of motion?

a) Force = Mass x Acceleration (F = MA)

b) More Leverage = More Force

c) $E = MC^2$

D) Fulcrum + Effort = Motion

Q12 – How many vertebrae in the spine?

a) 11

b) 22

c) 33

d) 44

Q13 – What is the term for a 1st degree black belt?

a) Shodan

b) Sandan

c) Nidan

4) Yondan

Q14 – The Japanese seated position is called:

a) Yōi

b) Matte

c) Seiza

d) Mushin

Q15 – The Japanese term for resuscitation techniques is:

a) CPR

b) Kappō

c) Seiza

d) Daisho

Q16 – Jūjutsu arrived to Britain in the:

a) 1900's

b) 1910's

c) 1920's

d) 1930's

Q17 – Ligaments hold muscles to:

a) Muscle

b) Bone

c) Joints

d) Skin

Q18 – The Japanese word for etiquette is:

a) Yame

b) Rei

c) Reshiki

d) Seiza

Q19 – The warrior 'way' is called:

a) Bujutsu

b) Jūjutsu

c) Budō

d) Tatami

Q20 – The artery in the neck is called the:

a) Radial

b) Femoural

c) Carotid

d) Bracial

Anatomy Exam:

Fill in the gaps on:

1) Bones

2) Muscles

3) Respiratory System

Skeletal System Test

Figure 42 – Skeletal system shodan test

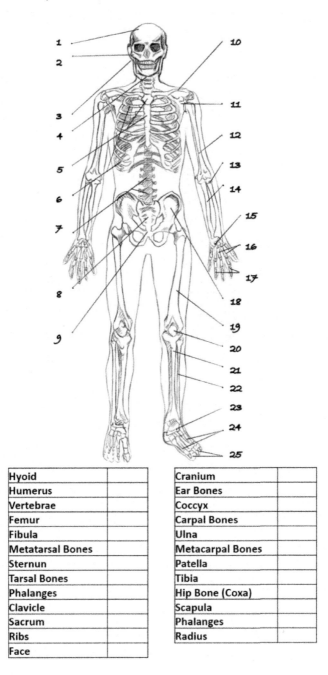

Hyoid		Cranium	
Humerus		Ear Bones	
Vertebrae		Coccyx	
Femur		Carpal Bones	
Fibula		Ulna	
Metatarsal Bones		Metacarpal Bones	
Sternun		Patella	
Tarsal Bones		Tibia	
Phalanges		Hip Bone (Coxa)	
Clavicle		Scapula	
Sacrum		Phalanges	
Ribs		Radius	
Face			

Spinal System Test

Figure 43 – Spinal system shodan test

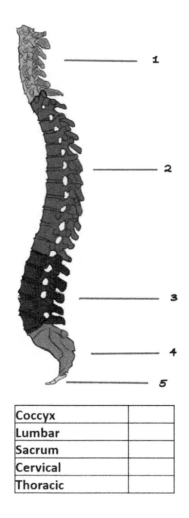

Coccyx	
Lumbar	
Sacrum	
Cervical	
Thoracic	

Muscular System Test

Figure 44 – Muscular system shodan test

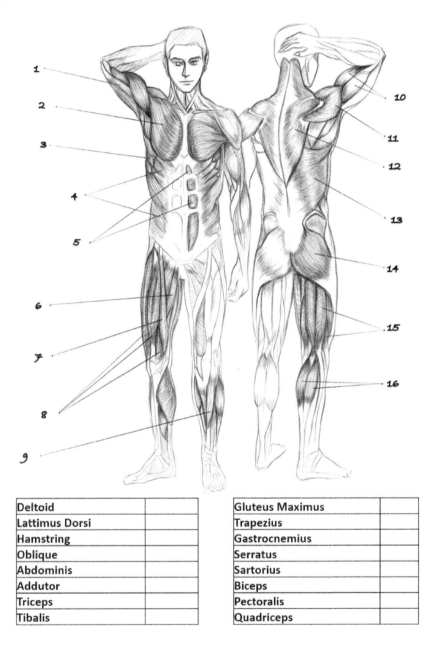

Deltoid			Gluteus Maximus	
Lattimus Dorsi			Trapezius	
Hamstring			Gastrocnemius	
Oblique			Serratus	
Abdominis			Sartorius	
Addutor			Biceps	
Triceps			Pectoralis	
Tibalis			Quadriceps	

Respiratory System Test

Figure 45 – Respiratory system shodan test

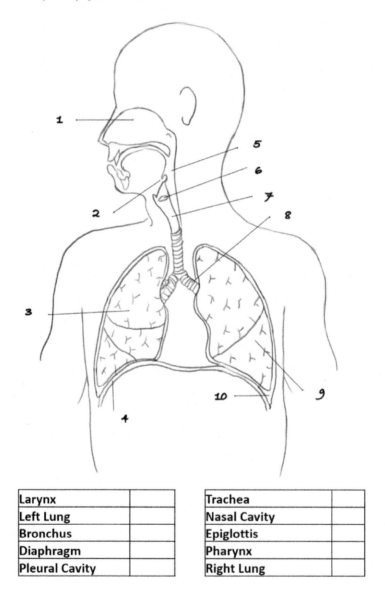

Larynx			Trachea	
Left Lung			Nasal Cavity	
Bronchus			Epiglottis	
Diaphragm			Pharynx	
Pleural Cavity			Right Lung	

Appendices

Translations

Table 33 – Japanese to English translations

Asu	Verb to harmonise or bring together
Age	Rising
Ago	Jaw
Ago-uchi	A strike to the jaw
Ai hamni	Mirrored Stance
Aiki	Harmony with energy or spirit
Aikidō	Martial art founded by Morihei Ueshiba
Akijutsu	Style of aikidi descended from Daitō ryū jiu jitsu
Ae	Opponent or adversary
Anza	Sitting cross-legged
Ashi-Ate	Art of attacking vital spots with the foot
Ashi	Leg or foot
Atemi	Vital or weak areas of the body (striking points)
Atemi-waza	Striking techniques
Ayumi-ashi	Ordinary step
Bajutsu	Art of horse riding
Bakufu	Yoritomo Minmoto's military government
Battō	To draw and cut with a blade
Bō	Wooden staff 5' to 6' long
Bō naginata	Wooden pole arm
Bō tantō	Wooden knife (for training)
Bōjutsu	Art of the Bō
Bogyo	Defence
Bokken	Wooden sword resembling a katana
Boshi	Thumb
Bu	Military or martial affairs
Bujutsu	All Japanese martial arts
Budō	Martial ways
Budōka	A student of the martial arts
Bugei	Japanese martial arts or skills
Bugeisha	A student of bugei

Buki	Weapons
Buki-hō	Weapon techniques/methods
Bujin	Low ranking samurai
Bushi	Samurai
Bushidō	The way of the samurai
Butsukari	Half way throwing practice
Chi	Earth
Chiburu	Ritualised shaking of sword for blood removal
Chikara	Strength
Chūdan	Middle-grade
Chunden	Mid-level
Dachi	Stance
Dai	Large
Dai kinniku	Major muscle
Dai nippon butokukai	Martial arts organisation established in Kyoto in 1895
Daichō	Large Intestine
Daishō	Pair of swords worn by a *samurai*
Daitai	Thigh
Dan	Black belt rank
Debana	To attack on movement
Denbu	Buttocks
Denko	Floating ribs (*atemi* point)
Deshi	Student
Do	The trunk of the body
Dō	The way
Dōjō	Training hall
Dokko	Pressure point behind the ear
Enpi	Elbow strike
Enpi-waza	Elbow techniques
En Sho	Round heel
Enga osae	Pinning face down
Eri	Lapel or collar
Fudōshin	Imperturbability of mind
Fuku shidōin	Instructor's assistant
Fukushiki kokyo	Abdominal breathing
Fukutō	Atemi point above the knee

Fumi-komi	Stepping in
Fumikomi age-uke	Stepping rising block technique
Funakoshi, Gichin	Name of Shotōkan Karate founder
Fusegi	Defence
Futari-waza	Two man attacks
Gaeshi	Reverse
Gaiwan	Outer edge of the arm
Ganmen	The face
Garami	Wrapping or entangling
Garami-waza	Entanglement techniques
Gedan	Lower level
Gei	Skill
Gekon	Pressure point at the lower lip
Gekyū	Low level kyū rank
Geri	Kick
Gi	Skill
Gi	Uniform
Gokoku	Pressure point between the finger/thumb
Goshin jutsu	Self-defence or a modern jūjutsu system
Gyakon	Pressure point on radial nerve
Gyō	Primary training stage
Hadaka	Naked
Hantei	Decision
Hara	Stomach or abdomen
Hidari	Left
Hikiwaki	Drawn contest
Hishigi	Crush, break or lock
Iaido	Way of drawing sword instantly
Ippon	One point
Jigai	Japanese ritual suicide method
Jigorō Kanō	Founder of Kōdōkan jūdō
Jigotai	Self defence posture
Jin	Person or human
Jinō	Kidneys
Jintai	The body
Jitsu	Art or skill

Jiu no michi	Path of gentleness
Jō	Wooden staff 4' long
Jō	Upper
Jō jutsu	Stick fighting art
Jōdan	Head level
Jōnin	Ninja leader
Jū	gentle/pliable/flexible
JūJutsu	Gentle Art
Jūdō	The gentle way
Juji	Cross
Jūnanshin	Correct attitude in training
Jutsu	Art or skill
Kajutsu	Explosive techniques
Kaeshi-waza	Counter techniques
Kai	Society, federation or association
Kaiken	Short dagger
Kaiten	Turning or spinning
Kakato	Heel
Kata	Posture
Kamae	Posture and stance
Kan	House or hall
Kansetsu-waza	Joint manipulation techniques
Kansetsute	Technique of bone and joint securing and breaking
Karate	Empty hand
Kata	Shoulder
Kata	Series of formalised techniques
Katame-waza	Grappling techniques
Katana	*Samurai* long sword
Katate	Empty hand
Katsu	Winning or being victorious
Kenpō	Iron fist
Ken	Fist
Ken	Blade
Kendo	Sporting method using wooden bokken
Kengo	Sword master
Kenjutsu	Japanese sword arts
Keppan	Blood seal

Ki	Inner strength or spirit
Ki o mitsuru	The assumption of a correct position, with the mind on the alert
Kiai	Unification and expression of energy
Kiaijutsu	Art used to develop *kiai*
Kihon	Basics
Kihon kumite	Basic sparring
Ko	Minor
Ko shi	Ball of foot
Ko soto gari	Minor outer reaping throw technique
Ko uchi gari	Minor inner reaping throw technique
Kobo jutsu	The art of ancient weaponry
Kōdōkan	World jūdō headquarters in Tokyo
Kokyu	Breathing
Koppo jutsu	Bone breaking techniques
Koroshi	Deathblow
Koshiki no kata	Ancient *kata* form of jūdō
Kote gaeshi	Wrist turning technique
Ku	Nine
Kubi	Neck
Kubu nage	Neck throw technique
Kuchi	Mouth
Kuchibiru	Lips
Kurai	A quiescent state of mind
Kuzushi	The breaking of the opponents' balance
Ko	Boy
Kyū	Grades lower than *dan* ranks
Kyūjutsu	Classical art of Japanese archery
Kyō	Modern Japanese archery art
Ma	Distance
Mā	Combat engagement distance
Mae	Front/forward
Maegeri	Front kick technique
Maetobigeri	Jumping front kick technique
Mae ukemi	Front break fall technique
Magotto	State of ego-less mind
Maitta	Exclamation "i give in"

Maki	Wrapped around
Makimono	Aincent Japanese hand scroll
Makikomi	Winding
Makiwara	Striking boards
Matte	Stop
Mawashi	Rotating turn
Mawatte	Turn around
Me	Eyes
Meijin	A person achieving physical, mental and spiritual perfection of their art
Men	Head or face
Men-kyo-kai-den	Teaching licence
Metsubushi	To throw ashes in the eyes' a blinding *atemi* strike
Michi	The way (same as '*dō*')
Migi	Right
Mimi	Ears
Mochi	To hold with the hands
Momo	Thigh
Mon	Japanese crest
Montei	Disciple or pupil
Morote	Using both hands
Mune	Chest
Muga-mushin	Maintain a composted posture in the face of attack
Mudansha	Coloured belt grade (below black belt)
Mushin	A 'flow' state of mind
Nagashi	Flowing
Nagashi-waza	Flowing techniques
Nage	Throw
Naginata	Pole arm weapon
Naifu	Knife
Naka	Middle or centre
Nakadaka	Middle knuckle
Nesshin	Zeal / enthuaism / fervor
Newaza	Groundwork
Nihon also Nippon	Native name for 'Japan'
Ninja	Japanese assassin or spy

Ninja-tō	Straight-bladed sword
Ninjutsu	The art of stealth/invisibility/assassination
Ninpō	The ninja way
Nodo	Throat
Nukite	Spear hand technique
Nunchaku	Wooden chained weapon
Nyūmon suru	To become a pupil / join the dōjō
Ō	Great or major
Ō goshi	Major hip throw technique
Ō guruma	Major wheel technique
Ō sensei	Great teacher
Ō soto gari	Major outer reaping throw technique
Ō uchi gari	Major inner reaping throw technique
Obi	Belt
Obi otoshi	Belt lifting drop technique
Okuden	Secret techniques
Osae	Immobilise
Osaekomi	Recognising a hold down in jūdō
Osae-waza	Immobilisation techniques
Osaeru	Verb to restrain
Randori	Free style sparring
Ranotori	Freedom of body movement
Rei	Bow
Renshu	Hard work
Renzoku	Combination techniques
Ritsu Rei	Standing bow
Rōnin	samurai warrior with no lord
Ryote dori	Holding both hands
Ryū	Style, art or school
Ryūgi	School / system
Sabaki	Body motion
Samurai	One who serves
Satori	Buddhist term for state of enlightenment
Saya	Scabbard
Seika tanden	Lower abdomen
Seiken	Fore fist
Seikichu	The spine

Seiza	Sitting position for abdominal breathing
Senpai	Senior student
Senaka	Back
Senjutsu	Tactics
Sensei	Teacher or instructor
Sensei ni rei	Bow to the teacher
Seppuku	Japanese ritual suicide
Shiai	Contest
Shiatsu	Japanese acupressure massage
Shidachi	The defender in kata
Shihan	Senior instructor
Shiho	Four directions
Shime	Choking
Shin	Heart
Shinai	Kendo bamboo sword
Shintai	The body
Shisei	Posture
Shodan	First level black belt grade
Shōgun	General (military rank)
Shōmen	Front
Shuriken	Throwing stars
Shuto	Knife edge hand
Sode	Sleeve
Sode dori	Sleeve grab technique
Sōji	The cleaning of the dōjō
Sojutsu	Spear art
Sōke	Head of family and head of style
Sokei	Groin
Sokuso	Tips of the toes
Sokutei	Bottom of the heel
Sokuto	Edge of the foot
Soto	Outer or outside
Suigetsu	Solar plexus
Sukui	Scooping
Sumi	Corner
Suwatte	Sit down
Tabi	Shoes or socks divided at the big toe

Tachi	Standing
Tai	Body
Taiatari	Body hardening / bruising / toughening
Tan	Gallbladder
Tanden	Abdomen
Tanko	Bladder
Tantō	Knife / dagger
Tantōjutsu	Knife fighting arts
Tatami	Mat area
Te	Technique / hand / trick
Teisho	Palm heel
Tekubi	Wrist
Tenkan	To go to the outside
Tonfa	Wooden handled weapon
Tori	Defender
Toroi nage	Armour throws
Tsuki	Punch
Tsukuri	Destroying balance
Uchi	Strike / interior
Uchideshi	A live-in student
Uchimontei	Student who lives in at the dōjō
Ude	Arm
Uke	Attacker
Ukemi	Break falls
Uki	Floating
Ura	Back / reverse
Ushiro	Behind / rear
Uwagi	Uniform jacket
Waki	Armpit
Wan	Arm
Wanryoku	Using brute strength to execute a technique (as opposed to *waza*)
Wanto	Arm sword
Waza	Technique / trick / skill (the neat and finished performance) as opposed to *wanryoku*
Yama	Mountain
Yame	Stop

Yari	Spear
Yawara	Original name of jūjutsu
Yoi	Ready
Yoko	To the side
Yoroi	Armour
Yowai	Weak
Yowaki	Weak energy
Yūdansha	Black belt grades
Yubi	Finger
Yūki	Courage
Yukkuri	Slow
Yumi	A bow
Za	Sitting
Za rei	Kneeling bow
Zanshin	A state of awareness
Zazen	Method of meditation (sitting)
Zekken	Badge with name of dōjō on
Zen	Religion and philosophy
Zori	Japanese sandals
Zubon	Trousers

References

Table 34 – Literary references

Adams	Andy	(1968)	**Jujitsu Fights for Survival** Black Belt Magazine, March 1968
Arrington	George	(2010)	**Yawara** - The Hand Arts of Danzan-Ryū Jujitsu Apollo's Magazine, London
Bankier	William	(1905)	**Ju-Jitsu** – What it really is by 'Apollo'
Bresler	Richard	(2021)	**Worth Defending**; How Gracie Jiu-Jitsu Saved My Life Reproduced in Journal of Combative Sport (2003) from The Idler – London, October 1892, p281-286
Burgin	George	(1892)	**Japanese Fighting**; Self-Defence by Sleight of Body Independently Published
Caracena	Jose	(2017)	**Tenjin Shinyo Ryu JuJitsu**
Cheek	Bryan	(2013)	**Jukoshin Ryu Jiu-Jitsu** Budo International Publ Co
Clark	Robert	(1979)	**World Ju Jitsu Federation Programme** Master Media
Clark	Robert	(1988)	**Masters' Jiu Jitsu** Penguin Group, London
Clark and Morris		(1985)	**Samurai Budo** - Ken-Jutsu_Kobu-Jutsu
Collingridge	W.H.	(1915)	**Tricks of Self-Defence** Athletic Publications Ltd, London
Corcoran and Farkas		(1983)	**Martial Arts** – Traditions, History, People Gallery Books, New York
Davies	Paul JL	(1989)	**Traditional and Modern Ju-Jitsu** Peterson Publishing, Worcs
Dean	Roy	(2013)	**The Martial Apprentice**

Dixon	Martin	(2003)	**Ju-Jitsu**

Amazon, ebook

Crowood Press, Wiltshire

Draeger	Donn	(1973)	**Classical Bujutsu**

John Weatherhill Inc, New York

Ettig	Wolfgang	(2004)	**Takamatsu Toshitsugu** – The Last Shinobi

Tengu Publishing, Germany

Fairbairn	W	(1942)	**Get Tough** – how to win in hand to hand fighting

, New York D Appleton-Century Company

Fairhurst	Derek	(1991)	**Ju Jutsu** – The Science The Art

Keenprint, Clwyd

Galan	Doru	(2014)	**Ju-jitsu as a method of psycho-physical training in the contemporary age**

Journal of physical activities 2014, Issue 3, P71

Garrud	W	(1914)	**The Complete Jujitsuan**

Methuen & CO LTD, London

Glossop	Reginald	(1907)	**Sunshine and Battle-Smoke**

A Brown & Sons, Hull

Gluck	Jay	(1974)	**Zen Combat**

Ballatine Books, New York

Goodger	Brian Christopher	(1981)	**The Development of Judo in Britain: A Sociological Study**

Ph.D Thesis, University of London

Gracie	Helio	(2005)	**Gracie Jiu-Jitsu**

Gracie Publications, California

Gracie	Rickson	(2021)	**Breathe,** a life in flow

Harper Collins

Hammond	Dave	(2008)	**Ippon!** The Fight for Judo's Soul

CPI Antony Rowe, Eastbourne

Hancock	Irving	(1904)	**Jiu Jitsu Combat Tricks**

Putnam's, London

Handcock and Higashi		(1938)	**The Complete Kano Jiu-Jitsu**

Putnam, London

Harrison	E	(1932)	**The Art of Ju-Jitsu**

W.Foulsham & Co, London

Harrison	E	(1950)	**The Fighting Spirit of Japan** W Foulsham & CO LTD, London
Hatsumi	Masaaki	(2013)	**Unarmed Fighting Techniques of the Samurai** Kodansha USA Inc, New York
Hunter	Harry	(1927)	**Super Ju-Jitsu** European Ju-Jitsu Association, Liverpool
Japan Society		(1892)	**Transactions and Proceeding of the Japan Society, London** Keegan Paul, Trench, Trubner and CO, Limited, London
Jay	Wally	(1994)	**Dynamic JuJitsu** Masters Publication, Ontario
Keegan	Simon	(2019)	**Bushido – A complete History of British Jujutsu** New Haven publishing Ltd
Kuboyama	Kazuhiko	(2015)	**The 'Mind-Set' of Jujutsuka in the Edo period in Japan as described in five historical documents (scrolls) from the Yoshin-ryū jujitsu school** Journal of Martial Arts Anthropology, Vol 14 Issue 4, p26
Lee	Bruce	(1975)	**The Tao of Jeet Kune Do** Ohara Publications, California
Lewis	Archibald	(1974)	**Knights & Samurai** Maurice Temple Smith Ltd, London
Liderman	Earle	(1923)	**The Science of Wrestling and the Art of Jiu Jitsu** Earle Liderman, New York
Longhurst	Percy	(1929)	**Ju-Jutsu and Judo** Frederick Warne & CO LTD, London & New York
Mclaglan	Leopold	(1922)	**Police Jiu Jitsu** The Police Review Publishing CO, London
Minami & Koyama	A & K	(1916)	**Spaldings Jiu-Jitsu** British Sports Publishing Company, London
Miyake & Tani	Taro & Yukio	(1905)	**The Game of Ju-jitsu** Hazell, Watson and Viney Ltd, London
Moclair	James	(2009)	**Ju-Jutsu - a Comprehensive Guide** AuthorHouse UK Ltd, Milton Keynes

Mol	Serge	(2001)	**Classical Fighting Arts of Japan**
			Kodansha, New York
Max Craig	Darrell	(2015)	**Japanese Jiu Jitsu**
			Tuttle Publishing North Clarendon
Musashi	Miyamoto	(2012)	**A Book of Five Rings**
			Translation by Victor Harris, Allison & Bushby, London
Norman	F.J.	(1905)	**The Fighting Man of Japan: The Training and Exercises of the Samurai**
			Archibald Constable &Co Ltd, London
Nakae & Yeager		(1959)	**Jiu Jitsu Complete**
			Lyle Stuart, New York
O'Brien	John	(1906)	**The Japanese Secret Science - Jiu Jitsu**
			Physicians' Publishing Company, Boston, US
Ohashi	M	(1912)	**Jiu Jitsu** – The Japanese System of Physical Culture
			Fox Publishing, New York
Pell	Kevin	(2008)	**Martial Art Basics - Ju-Jitsu**
			Grange Books, Kent
Petermann	Hans-Erik	(2004)	**Jiu Jitsu** - The Essential Guide to Mastering the Art
			New Holland, London
Rahming	D'Arcy	(1991)	**Combat Ju-Jutsu** - The Lost Art
			Modern Bu-Jutsu Inc, IL
Ratti and Westbrook	Oscar and Adele	(2009)	**Secrets of the Samurai** – The Martials Arts of Feudal Japan
			Tuttle Publishing, U.S.A
Redenbach	Robert	(2008)	**Waveman**
			Courtney Ballantyne Publishing, Australia
Ross	Robert G	(2005)	**JuJitsu**; the Essentials
			Trafford Publishing (UK) ltd, Oxford
Sainthilaire	R	(2021)	**Pioneers of American JuJitsu** American Jujitsu before WWII
			Amazon
Short and Hashimoto	James G and Katsuharu	(1979)	**Beginning Ju Jitsu Ryoi-Shinto Style**
			Donald & Co, London

Skinner	Capt Harry	(1904)	**Jiu-Jitsu** – The Japanese method of Attack and Defense
			The Baker & Taylor CO, New York
Stroud	Mike	(2004)	**Survival of the Fittest**
			Random House, London
Stevens	John	(1999)	**The Essence of Aikido**
			Kodansha International Ltd, Japan
Sutherland	Bruce	(1916)	**Ju-Jitsu Self-Defence**
			Thomas Nelson & Sons Ltd
Syed	Matthew	(2011)	**Bounce – The Myth of Talent and the Power of Practice**
			Harper Collins, London
Tedeschi	Marc	(2008)	**Essential Anatomy for Healing & Martial Arts**
			Weatherhill, Boston
Turnbull	Stephen	(2003)	**Samurai** - The World of the Warrior
			Osprey, Westminster
Uyenishi	Sadakazu	(1940)	**The Textbook of Ju-Jutsu as Practised in Japan**
			Athletic Publications, London
Wilson	Scott	(1982)	**Ideals of the Samurai** – Writings of Japanese Warriors
			Ohara Publications, USA
Watts & Beldam	Emily & G.W	(1906)	**The Fine Art of JuJutsu**
			William Heinemann, London
Woodman	Allen	(2014)	**History of Japanese Martial Arts**
			Sidekick Publications
Yiannakis	Andrew	(2017)	**JuJutsu** – Traditions, Ways and Modern Practices
			Belfort & Bastion

Table 35 – Web references

BJJA GB		(2019)	**About the BJJA GB**
			http://www.bjjagb.com/about/about-the-bjja-gb/ (Accessed: Feburary 2019)
Breen	Paul	(2012)	**A History of Ju-Jitsu**
			http://crosbyjujitsuacademy.blogspot.com/2012/10/ (Accessed: Feburary 2019)

Brough	Dave	(2018)	**The History of Bushido and British Ju Jitsu** https://knutsfordjuju.wordpress.com/2018/08/05/, (Accessed: Feburary 2019)
Crown Prosecution Service (CPS)		(2020)	**The Self-Defence and the Prevention of Crime** https://www.cps.gov.uk/legal-guidance/self-defence-and-prevention-crime (Accessed: April 2020)
Grant	T.P	(2016)	**Jiu-Jitsu History: Birth on the Battlefield** http://www.bloodyelbow.com/2011/10/13/2481689/jiu-jitsu-history-birth-on-the-battlefield (Accessed:March 2016)
Jitsu Foundation		(2016)	**Jitsu Foundation** https://www.jitsufoundation.org/ (Accessed:March 2016)
Judo Info		(2016)	**The Judo Rank System – Belts** http://judoinfo.com/obi.htm (Accessed:March 2016)
Keegan	Simon	(2010)	**British JuJutsu** http://www.e-budō.com/forum/showthread.php?45810-Research-into-British-Jujitsu/page2 (Accessed: Feburary 2019)
London JuJutsu		(2019)	**Richard Morris 10th Dan** http://www.londonjiujitsu.co.uk/index.php/richard-morris/
The Budokwai		(2016)	**102 Years of the Budokwai** http://budokwai.co.uk/history (Accessed:June 2016)
The Science Classroom		(2016)	**Martial Arts and Newton's Laws of Motion** https://thescienceclassroom.wikispaces.com/Martial+Arts+and+Newton%27s+Laws+of+Motion (Accessed:May 2016)
UKBJJA.org		(2022)	**BJJ in the UK and the formation of the UKBJJA** Ukbjja.org/about/
Wikipedia		(2016)	**Bushido, Keikogi, Kimono, Lever, Seiza** https://en.wikipedia.org (Accessed:March 2016)

List of Figures

List of Tables

List of Images

<u>Acknowledgements</u>

Thank you to my goshin jūjutsu sensei, Ian Woolston, for passing on his knowledge to myself and others who have benefited from his teaching:

The first rule of self-defence: ***Don't be there!*** 15
The second rule of self-defence: ***If it works, use it!*** 74

Figure 46 - Modern jūjutsuka throwing ancient samurai

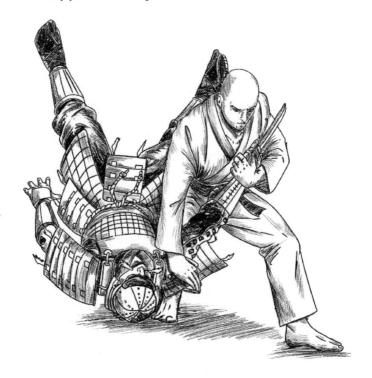

Figure 47 – Enso, representing the never-ending journey

If you enjoyed the book and have the opportunity to do so, please leave feedback on your retailers website, these reviews are very much appreciated.

Printed in Great Britain
by Amazon

42535879R00106